PREPARE NOW

10 PRACTICAL GUIDES TO SURVIVING & THRIVING DURING CRISES

NONSO OKPALA, CPA, MAcc, INHC

www.ktvahealth.com
email: info@ktvahealth.com

Names, characters, businesses, places, events, locales, and incidents are either the products of the author's imagination or used in a fictitious manner. Any resemblance to actual persons, living or dead, or actual events is purely coincidental.

The material contained in Prepare NOW is for general information and the purpose of educating individuals on ways to prepare for recessions and the personal crises that accompany them. The author is not engaged in rendering health, financial, legal or other professional service. Please seek the services of competent professionals if you require health, financial or legal advice.

ISBN: 978-1-7351-9140-9

Praise for **PREPARE NOW**

"Nonso makes a hit with a book that covers several of life's challenges that affect all of us. He truly has something for everyone, and he motivates us to take action to build a better life."

- **Thomas J. Phillips, Jr., Ph.D., CPA**, Professor of Accounting, Louisiana State University.

"Attention getting with tough love reality is what you get in Prepare NOW—10 Practical Guides to Surviving and Thriving During Crises. The book is well written and it provides practical alternatives for maintaining economic and family stability during financial recessions.

The author, Nonso Okpala, holds a Masters of Accountancy degree and is a Certified Public Accountant. During the current global financial crises and pandemic, Nonso serves as a Corporate Controller of a major Financial Institution.

Nonso emphasized the urgency of the NOW to survive when, not if, recessions and pandemics come. He uses a holistic approach that considers not only the reader financial status but also their personal health, mental and physical, and their spirituality. Nonso indicates "The greatest and most rewarding investment you can make is in your health, because everything you do in this life is done in or through your body."

Based upon the title of this book, Prepare NOW, it is somewhat obvious that the emphasis of the book would be placed on the NOW preparation. It is better to prepare when the economy is good and when life is "good." However, it is still appropriate to prepare even now when there is a global financial crisis caused in part from the current pandemic.

The author suggests to establish additional revenue streams to replace the reliance on a job revenue stream since businesses employment levels are based upon the financial condition of the economy. A lot of attention is given in the book to the various business models that use "what's in your hands" as to current technology and personal talents and interests to approach the creation of additional revenue sources. The book provides the reader with information about using financial strategies for "getting ahead" of financial crises before they occur or reoccur."

"Okpala provides illustrative examples to describe the importance of preestablishing community and financial support systems for not only economic recessions purposes but also for personal recessions necessities including health and spiritual reservoirs. These support systems are there to provide both mental and financial resources during recessions and/or pandemics when family and friends are likely the only support in living a "new norm." The author also indicates that it is better to NOW resize current styles of living before the financially stressed economy forces a downsizing. Readers are given tactics to take control of their financial destinies by implementing NOW doable preparation strategies for not only to survive but also to thrive during times of financial recessions.

Nonso defines recession "as the steep decline in domestic or global economic activities for a protracted period of time." He also introduces the concept of personal recession, "which transcends economic crisis."

Personal recession is anything that brings about major economic downturn or financial hardships to you for a prolonged period of time. In other words, conditions and circumstances that have the potential to put you in a bad financial position for unforeseeable periods of time, such as job loss, unexpected health challenges, marriage problems or permanent disability.

I highly recommend this book as a "must read" when considering how unprepared global nations and their citizens were during the current recession and pandemic. Plan NOW and avoid the fear, that comes from not being prepared, which may destroy families and futures during worldwide financial crises periods and equally important, during times of personal recessions."

- **Professor Carl N. Wright, Ph.D., CPA**, Accounting Professor, Colorado State University—Pueblo.

"Nonso Okpala writes with a prodigious skill in "Prepare Now" and strives to educate his readers on what changes they must take to live a recession-proof life. The chapters are easy to read, full of life and captivating. They convey, in lay man's terms, the resources and tools needed to avert pandemonium when (or if) recession hits! Happy Reading."

- **Dr. Tobe Momah, MD.**, founder, Faith and Power Ministries and author of *From Edginess to Eagerness*.

"Prepare NOW is a timely wake up call. Those who take Action NOW to implement these steps will be better prepared for your next personal recession. The book is full of practical, common sense, "the stuff your grandma used to say" guidelines however, these are things far too often overlooked or ignored at your own peril. Like the saying from old, "If you fail to plan, you are planning to fail!". I give this book 5 stars."

- **TJ Silvis**, Qualified Accountant.

This book is dedicated to six most important ladies in my life - the love of my life (Cynthia Okpala), my three precious kids (Ogo, Amara, & Uche Okpala), my sweet mother (Mercy Okpala), and my supportive godmother (Vera Malone). Without you, I would not have survived several personal recessions that I experienced at different stages of my life. To my sweetheart, thank you for not only supporting me but also taking care of most of the family's responsibilities during the time I was writing this book.

CONTENTS

FOREWORD

By Blaise Wabo

It was on a very cold morning at church in January 2007 that I met Nonso. I had just been in the U.S. for couple weeks, and even though I was used to being away from my parents and family (after going to boarding schools from the age of 11), this time was uniquely different because I was across the Atlantic Ocean almost 11,000 km (6,800 miles) away from home, and my parents could not visit easily during the holidays and school breaks. Being in a new country and new culture at the age of 18, I was desperate to make friends and have a sense of home. Once I met Nonso, I instantly felt a sense of home; he had a welcoming smile and a kind heart.

We exchanged contact information and started hanging together. We attended the same church and student ministry, and both pursued accounting degree. During the second semester in college, we decided to move off-campus and became roommates. For over 13 years, I still call Nonso my best friend and I do not cease to be amazed by his dedication to prepare and achieve great success. Nonso has always been a step ahead of everyone else and one of his favorite quotes is 'when preparation meets opportunity, success is inevitable'.

I can truly say that this is how Nonso has lived his life since the day I met him. He is the kind of guy that who will study ahead of time before a class, get his clothes ready for the next day and diligently do all his research before a major project. Nonso completed his undergraduate accounting degree in less than four years and immediately went to a graduate school, which he completed in less than 18 months. Passing the CPA exam after grad school was just a result of the 4 years of preparation. Staying laser focus with a passion for teaching, Nonso became one of the youngest professors of accounting in the history of the University where he taught. He then edited and published an accounting textbook that launched nationally.

Today, Nonso lives in Delaware with his beautiful wife and three daughters; he is a controller at a financial institution. He has always had a side hustle from being a travel agent in college, student assistant, tutor, blogger and vlogger with www.ktvahealth.com (his health and wellness business), to being a health and wellness coach. From the eastern part of Nigeria, raised as the youngest in the family by a poor single mom, to Investment Banking in the Mid-Atlantic state of Delaware where more than half of all the U.S. publicly traded companies and Fortune 500 companies are incorporated, Nonso marked his own destiny by 'Preparing Now' every day of his life.

When Nonso asked me to write the foreword for this book 'Prepare Now', it brought a lot of emotions to my heart not only because he is my best friend, but also because I am so proud of his accomplishments and I'm looking forward to celebrating many more. In this book, Nonso provides 10 practical guides for not only surviving but also thriving during any crisis. He uses real life stories, which are easily relatable by anyone as well as his personal experiences, to convey the message. I believe this book will not only challenge the readers to take action NOW, but also give them the tools necessary to start that journey. Nonso and I both graduated from college after the housing market crash and Great Recession of 2007 – 2009. We both experienced severe hardships, and I saw Nonso live these principles. He turned what could be a sad story into an All American dream while helping and inspiring others during that journey. 'Everything you do in this life is done in or through your body' is another quote Nonso likes, and in this book, Nonso provides a holistic approach to having a well-balanced life from the financial, health & wellness to spiritual perspective.

When I first read this book, I was on a plane to Chicago from Denver for the July 4th holiday and I could not drop the book until I finished reading it. The stories were captivating, thrilling and kept me on the edge of my seat. As the flight attendant said before we took off for Chicago, 'now is your last chance to de-plane from the aircraft if you do not want to go to Chicago.' So now is your last chance to drop this book because once you start reading it, it will change your life. Buckle-up and enjoy the ride.

My name is Blaise Wabo, CPA, CISA. I am currently a Director at A-LIGN, a CPA and Cybersecurity firm, providing strategic security and compliance services to companies worldwide. I am also a real-estate investor, entrepreneur, community leader, husband and father of two children (soon to be three). I currently live in Denver, CO and love reading, running and traveling.

CHAPTER 1

PREPARE NOW

"One of life's most painful moments comes when we must admit that we didn't do our homework, that we are not prepared." –Merlin Olson.

Scott was a 55-year-old managing director at an investment and hedge funds firm. He was born and raised in Houston, Texas and had never lived anywhere else (other when he was deployed overseas). The first thing you would see if you walked into Scott's office was a photo of him with his best friend, both in military regalia during one of his military assignments overseas. Scott was a decorated veteran and had served in the U.S. Army for 11 years before joining his firm in 1989.

Scott worked long hours, and sometimes, he worked on weekends. Just two years after joining the investment and hedge fund company, he got his first promotion. As promotions came, so did additional and challenging work. Although work became tough as he climbed the "corporate ladder", Scott was never deterred. After several years of working extremely hard, and sometimes under severe pressure and stress, Scott was promoted to managing director, a coveted and revered position that only few people attain in their career. As a managing director, Scott commanded a decent salary.

At the peak of his career, Scott earned a whopping $400,000 a year in salary and bonus. You didn't need him to tell you that he was earning a decent salary. Scott bought a $700,000 house six months after he became a managing director. He also owned a $60,000 fishing boat, and a $130,000 skiing boat. He loved to take his family on skiing expeditions. Except for a few minor health challenges, Scott was truly living the American dream. He had a beautiful family, okay health, a nice home, and a promising job that paid generously. Scott lacked nothing.

Suddenly, the winds of adversity blew along Scott's path, and they were damaging: The Great Recession of 2008. The "perfect" life that Scott had built for himself was put to the test. As the recession began to squeeze the U.S., Scott's company began to feel the pressure. As a top earner at the firm, Scott knew that there was a slight risk that his job could be affected. However, he was confident that his work ethic, expertise and wisdom would be needed to help his company survive the recession. Unfortunately, that did not happen. Sadly, Scott was caught in the crossfire. The company that he had called his own, a company to which he had dedicated a big part of his life, a company that he helped to become one of the top hedge funds companies in the world, decided to let him go. On January 29, 2008, Scott was fired.

He was devastated, discouraged, and demoralized. For the first time in his entire life, Scott felt helpless. He knew that at his managing director level, it would be tough to find a job within a short period of time. Eight months later, he was still looking for a job. The ability to maintain his normal lifestyle became a big struggle. Debts began to pile up. With no regular income in sight, the only option was to tap into his savings to pay for his home, cars, boats, and other expenses. Things became so bad financially that Scott had to sell his two boats and his second BMW. Faced with mounting debt and no job in sight, Scott became fearful and anxious. Anger and frustration began to build up.

Because he was in the military for a long time, he was the most disciplined person you would ever meet. He was known for his calmness in the face of danger. That was why Scott's wife became really worried when Scott began to yell at her and their children at the slightest provocation. His health also began to fail him. He had managed to control his blood sugar levels very well, but with the crisis facing him, Scott did not pay close attention to his health and stopped his regular doctor visits. As a result, his diabetes worsened, which resulted in amputation of his leg a year and two months after losing his job.

Life was never the same again for Scott. Currently, he teaches finance at a community college.

"A recession is a period in the business cycle when economic activities are in a general decline, typically accompanied by elevated unemployment, falling income and consumer spending, rising business failures, and falling stock markets."[1] I define recession as the steep decline in domestic or global economic activities for a protracted period of time. In this book, I introduce the concept of personal recession, which transcends economic crisis.

Personal recession is anything that brings about major economic downturn or financial hardships to you for a prolonged period of time. In other words, conditions and circumstances that have the potential to put you in a bad financial position for unforeseeable periods of time, such as job loss, unexpected health challenges, marriage problems or permanent disability, are personal recessions.

Around 2007 to 2009, when we had the financial market crisis, millions of people lost their jobs. Suicide rate skyrocketed. Divorce rate spiked. Families were in disarray. Alcohol abuse was at an all-time high. Drug overdoses became commonplace. Domestic violence and abuse increased. There is no doubt that experiencing recession has a way of changing people's lives for the worse, if proper precautions are not taken and if adequate plans are not in place to withstand the pressure that comes with experiencing a personal financial crisis.

Preparation is key to surviving any recession. In a broader sense, there are many factors that can trigger what is known as recession. However, we will focus on how recession affects you personally. More specifically, we will look at how recession can lead to personal crises, especially personal financial crisis. So, as you read this book, think of recession in a much broader sense - personal recession, national or global recession. They all have the tendency to impact your financial wellbeing adversely.

Obviously, recession does not last forever, but the impact can if you fail to plan way in advance before it happens. Again, think about the impact of the 2008-2009 recession. The world economy contracted. Many people lost their jobs, and others lost their lives. By 2010, things began to turn around. The economy began to experience expansion again. Sadly, not everyone experienced expansion in their own personal life and finance. For some, even ten years later, they are still struggling from the financial impact of the Great Recession. Why did some recover fast and others didn't? Why did some people experience little to no impact at all? It boils down to preparation.

This book will help you understand why you should prepare now to protect yourself from crises brought on by any recession. You will learn how to prepare now in order to withstand the pressure that comes with crisis. Regardless of the type of recession, preparation is vital if you ever want to survive and thrive when it comes your way. It's not if, but when. You don't wait until recession strikes before you swing into action. You should plan for it way in advance. Whether you will recover depends on whether you prepared in advance and how you prepared for such hard times. Scott failed to devise a strategy to protect himself against recession. As a result, he lost virtually everything owned, including his health.

WHY YOU MUST PREPARE FOR RECESSION NOW

The impact of the Great Recession is unquantifiable. While individuals from diverse backgrounds, cultures and races experienced varying degrees of hardships, men and minorities suffered the most. One study found that the Great Recession led to a decline in fertility and low birthweights in newborn babies. That same study found that more Black and Hispanic households had foreclosed homes and increased health issues than any other groups.[2] Unemployment, financial hardship and foreclosures led to increased underlying health conditions.

The recession also led to increased mental health problems, particularly among Black and Hispanic individuals. A research study found that the United States, Europe and Canada had an increase in post-recession suicide rates, which were mainly attributed to job losses and housing related issues. Sadly, the suicide rates were higher among "working-aged men".[3] Excessive alcohol drinking and other alcohol related problems resulting from loss of jobs and foreclosures, significantly increased among blacks and men.[4] As you might have guessed, financial struggles affect one's ability to buy healthy foods. People purchased more high-calorie foods as well as fast foods and soft drinks.[5]

One of the biggest challenges we deal with as human beings is that we are too quick to forget. Once we get out of a crisis and things settle back to normal, we forget and live our normal lives. Don't get me wrong, you should not spend every single day thinking about what you experienced in the past. But you have to clearly define what happened, why it happened, and how you survived. How did the last recession crisis impact you? Did you suffer for a long time? Did you barely make it out alive? Did you experience a minor scratch, a bruise or a very deep wound from the impact of the personal recession? Asking and answering these questions can help you determine why you went through the crisis, what you learned from it, and what to do now to avoid such a crisis in the future.

I recall a story of a gentleman who lost his job during the Great Recession. That singular experience led him to create his own company. Today, his business is thriving and he is helping others come out of the personal financial crisis. Those who fail to learn from their bitter past experience are bound to witness it again. If you can't answer these questions clearly, you probably moved on with your life without learning anything from your past recession.

You must prepare while your personal or the global economy is booming. You must prepare while the stock market is at an all-time high. You must prepare while your investment portfolios are looking awesome. You must prepare while you have a nice home, cars and other assets. You must prepare while your marriage is thriving and your kids are well-behaved. You must prepare while you're at the zenith of your career. And you must prepare while you feel great in your body. You know why? Any of these things can flip on you in a split second. Don't wait until tomorrow.

Take the COVID-19 pandemic for example. Think about its impact on the global economy. The United States economy was as best as it could be before the pandemic. Dow Jones Industrial Average was nearing 30,000 points as of January 2020.[6] Suddenly, COVID-19 struck and in just a few months the United States economy was dragged to its knees. The world economy almost came to a grinding halt. Businesses began to shut down. People started losing their jobs. Fear gripped many hearts. Stress and anxiety began to intrude.

If you have the right mix of preparation and anticipation, it will be easier to manage the unanticipated and unintended impacts of a recession. There are three key benefits of preparing for personal financial crisis now:

1. Preparation minimizes fear during financial crisis

FEAR is one of the biggest threats to surviving any major personal financial crisis. Do you know what the antidote for fear is? PREPARATION. If you have prepared adequately for a crisis, and have put measures in place to tackle it, you don't need to fear. Once the next recession hits, you can swing into action immediately. You pull out everything in your arsenal and attack, overcome, defeat, and win.

Let's say your personal recession is the loss of a job. To cope with the stress and anxiety of losing your job, you start to drink alcohol in excess. Consequently, you start to abuse your spouse or kids. What might happen? You might go to jail. You might lose your marriage. You might permanently lose your relationship with your kids. None of this will bring your job back. You see, adequate preparation is crucial if you want to survive any financial hardship that results from experiencing recession in your life.

On a positive note, if you prepare ahead of time and do it well, you will not have a reason to fear. If you ever face a recession, you won't make impulsive decisions that have the potential to derail your life, your family, and your future. Instead, your focus will be on implementing the processes that you have already developed.

2. Preparation improves your confidence during financial crisis

If you're a sports fan, you understand and appreciate how much time players spend practicing in preparation for a major game – say, the Super Bowl or Champions League final. Players spend countless hours preparing, both as a team and individually. They strategize. They study their opponents to understand their strengths and weaknesses. Players don't wait until a day before or on the day of the big game to prepare.

You should apply the same logic to any financial struggles that recession causes.

On the day of the final game, players' confidence lies in the fact that they have spent a good amount of time preparing to defeat and win their opponent. They go into the game with one goal in mind: Execute! Players are confident that once they execute their plans, they have a high chance of winning the game.

It's one thing is to have a plan, but another to execute it well. The team that fails to execute their plan may suffer a great loss at the hand of their opponent. Also, a team that deviates from plans that have been tested and proven to be effective may also suffer a defeat. Prepare ahead of time for any potential personal recessions, and execute, execute, execute when crisis strikes. Have confidence that your tested and trusted plans will work 100 percent of the time.

Just like players can adjust how to execute their prepared plans if there is a need, you should be flexible enough to adjust your strategy during a recession. But you must be careful not to deviate from the plans that actually work. Fear drives people to deviate from executing plans even after they have prepared well. Fear is irrational, and irrational decisions lead to failure to execute well-prepared plans.

Prepare. Trust your plans. Preparation not only builds your confidence, it also gives you an assurance that your plans will work even in the most difficult financial situation.

3. Preparation provides assurance that personal recession is temporary

There is nothing as heartwarming and refreshing as seeing the light at the end of the tunnel. Imagine falling into a dark cave. When you cry out for help, all you hear is the reverberation of that cry. And suddenly you hear a voice, accompanied by a tiny light. That voice and light provide assurance that your days in the dark won't last for too long. It may take a while before help arrives but you have the assurance that it will come. Experiencing a recession is like being in a dark cave. Preparing for a recession in advance is like the voice and light assuring you that help is on the way. Those who sink into despair during a crisis have no hope of surviving. They feel hopeless and helpless, and they lose the zeal to fight.

This is why so many people crumble under the pressure of crisis. When you prepare in advance, you have the assurance that the hardship that comes with recession won't last forever. You know you have prepared well and that with your plans properly executed, you will outlast your recession. Preparation is the light that shines at the end of the tunnel, signaling that the end of your crisis is in sight.

PREPARE NOW, NOT TOMORROW

It's important to note that the national or global economy could be doing well even as your own economy is not. Conversely, the economy could be going through a recession while your own economy is thriving. In fact, you could be experiencing the biggest expansion of your life while the global economy is in bad shape. It all begins with preparation. Coincidentally, the global or national recession could trigger a personal recession.

In any case, if you have solid plans in place or the right process in place, if you've prepared adequately, if you stick to the plan and execute well when a recession strikes – global or personal – you have no reason to fear. You have no reason to go into panic mode, and surely you have no reason to give up hope. You will not only survive, but thrive during any crisis.

The following chapters will guide you through how to prepare for any personal financial crisis that recession could trigger. These practical guides will equip you with everything you need to withstand the nastiest recession you can ever face. As you navigate each chapter, you will notice that each chapter title ends with "now". This is very important. Procrastination is the enemy to preparation. Procrastinators push everything to tomorrow.

Now is the right time to prepare. Now is the right time to take action. Now is the right to hone your plans. Now is the right time to test your plans. Not tomorrow. If you procrastinate and push everything to tomorrow, before you know it tomorrow will be here and that tomorrow might be D-Day-the day recession invades your personal life unannounced. You could find yourself scrambling for solutions. You could become defenseless. Do not allow your current economic status to deceive you.

Ask any well-established business professionals who lost pretty much everything during the Great Recession. Ask the sole provider in a home who underwent a serious health crisis that wiped out all their sources of income. I'm sure they'll tell you that if they had prepared a lot better and sooner, their financial struggles that followed their recessions would not have been so severe. I believe Scott would concur that if he had managed his debt better, he probably would not have suffered as severely. You saw in Scott's story that he not only commanded a decent salary, but also had a reasonable savings. Unfortunately, he amassed such enormous debt that his savings alone only sustained him for a period of time. The longer your recession the more severe the financial hardship could become. Consider each chapter in this book as an essential tool that you must have in your toolbox. Each tool will serve a different purpose during recession.

I urge you to take this very seriously. Start from somewhere – wherever you can – and continue to build upon it. The only thing you can't afford to do is nothing. It will cost you more than you bargained for. My hope is that by the time you finish reading this book, you can pick out several guides that you can start applying in your personal life.

The Great Recession almost destroyed Scott's life. It took everything from him that meant so much, including his health.

You can learn from Scott's experience. Now is the time to invest in things that will sustain you when recession knocks on your door. NOW IS THE TIME!

CHAPTER 2

BE YOUR OWN BOSS NOW

"To dream anything that you want to dream – that is the beauty of the human mind. To do anything you want to do – that is the strength of the human will. To trust yourself to test your limits – that is the courage to succeed." –Bernard Edmonds.

Single and super narcissistic. That is Bobby. Bobby is a 42-year-old store manager at a popular high-end clothing store in Paradise Valley, Arizona. Everyone in the city calls him Bobby Bling-Bling because he is well known for his flashy and extravagant lifestyle.

Customers who visit the clothing store where Bobby works often mistake him for a celebrity rapper due to his appearance. Bobby values his physical appearance more than he values his own life. He always goes to extreme lengths to impress himself and others, even if that means living beyond his means. In short, Bobby is the embodiment of a facade.

Although he makes $95,000 a year, Mr. Bling-Bling drives a Mercedes Benz E-Class and lives in a $550,000 house. He owns seven different colognes and he wears one for each day of the week. But that's not all; he also owns seven different gold watches, gold chains, and gold rings, one for each day of the week.

Bobby's ability to maintain his lavish lifestyle was tested in February 2019. As more shoppers turned to the internet, Bobby's company began to feel the heat. Then came the unexpected emergency meeting.

Bobby's boss told him the company was downsizing and was given a choice: take a 30% pay cut or find another job elsewhere. Bobby lifted his head up, stared his boss in the face for about 10 seconds and mumbled, "I'll take the pay cut".

You would expect Bobby to start experiencing some financial hardship. After all, it would be almost impossible for him to maintain his extravagant lifestyle on a $67,000 salary. Then came another mind-blowing move: two months after receiving a pay cut, Bobby sold his home in Phoenix and bought a home in Paradise Valley – a much more expensive city – for $840,000.

Why would Bobby take a pay cut and then buy an expensive home? Only a few people know it, but Bobby does not depend on his $67K salary to sustain himself or his extravagant lifestyle. Bobby's regular job gives him the opportunity to interact with hundreds of customers; it also enables him to stay informed about clothing trends, which he leverages to promote trending brands on his YouTube channel. His appearance makes him stand out wherever he goes, and he takes full advantage of the attention that he receives to build his own online brand. Mr. Bling-Bling does not sell a single physical product but, on average, he generates over $30,000 a month. His model is simple: vlogging.

But how did Bobby get to the point where he commands over $30,000 in revenue? In a word, "experience." Experience, they say, is the best teacher, and Bobby had his fair share of experiences he never wants to repeat.

Bobby holds a master's degree in tourism and hospitality. Before 2008, he was considered the rising star in the tourism industry. He was the hospitality director at a famous resort in Florida. His unique ways of dressing have always endeared him to people, including notable media outlets and popular travel magazines. In 2006, Bobby was featured in a national travel magazine as the one of the future faces of tourism.

But all that recognition and aspiration came crashing down in the spring of 2008. The tourism industry suffered greatly during the recession, and Bobby's job was affected. He lost his job, his home and his car. At the lowest point of his life, Bobby had to make a choice: remain homeless and rot away, or sell his pride and seek help.

Bobby's parents had to send him a bus ticket to travel from Orlando, Florida to Phoenix, Arizona. While living with his parents, Bobby began to hash out plans to get out of the financial mud that he was in. In the end, it boiled down to one thing: building something that would be recession-proof. Bobby began to leverage the internet and his personality to build his brand. He started a YouTube channel where he talks about his personal life, as well as entertainment, luxury clothing brands, hospitality and tourism. In a few short years, Bobby grew his audience. The more his audience grew, the more businesses vied for a spot to promote their products on Bobby's channel.

In 2015, he left his parents' home and bought his own house. As things continued to improve for him, Bobby sought new ways to monetize his YouTube popularity. In 2016, he developed an online course - "How to Tour the World on A Budget." The online course continues to generate thousands of dollars each year in passive income. Indeed, Bobby's quest to become recession-proof seems to have paid off.

Becoming a business owner can be a challenging, yet rewarding venture. Too many people have great ideas they can potentially turn into a business. But only a few step out to develop those ideas and turn them into business ventures. Do you know why? It's one word: FEAR.

Fear keeps many people from starting a business. What if the business fails? What if there is not enough profit from the business to take care of personal financial needs? Or I don't think I have the right experience and qualifications to become a business owner. Fear-induced questions like these keep many brilliant minds from turning their lucrative ideas into thriving and profitable businesses. They would rather get jobs that guarantee a monthly paycheck rather than start a business that does not guarantee any success.

In other words, fear can keep you from stepping out of your comfort zone. We celebrate great inventions by people who did not allow fear to keep them from taking a leap of faith to try something new. We celebrate them because they succeeded and because they never gave up even when things looked bleak or when it appeared they would not succeed.

Now is the time to start and grow your business. If you're worried about having a safety net, you can still own a small business while working your full-time job. Of course, your ultimate goal should be to transition full-time to your business at some point, but there are some full-time jobs that may provide the flexibility to do both temporarily. A powerful problem-solving business idea combined with the world of the internet provides you a great prospect of succeeding if you launch your business now. You will never know if your ideas can turn into a successful and profitable business until you try.

A NOTE FOR BUSINESS OWNERS

If you currently own a business, you should go a step further and ask yourself one pertinent question: would my business survive any major crisis? If the answer is yes, you must ask a follow up question: during a recession, would my income decline to the point that I would struggle to keep the lights on? If you answered yes, keep reading because there are few tips that I will share in this chapter that you can leverage to create multiple streams of income. If you answered no, then you need to figure out how to build a fortress around your business so it can withstand financial pressure that comes with recession.

TAKE YOUR BUSINESS ONLINE

If you have a business idea, why not develop it now? You just have to get creative. What are you good at? Do you currently own a business? Whether you're an established professional – such as a professor, plumber, electrician or hairdresser – or a hobbyist painter, designer or photographer, there is a way to take your business to the next level.

Leverage the internet to grow and profit from your business. Use social media platforms to showcase your business and your talent. If you're a painter or a barber, use YouTube to show the world your expertise and technique. If you're a photographer or hairdresser, use Instagram to market your skills. If you're a professor or writer, create a blog or website to create content relevant to your field or interests.

When you bring your business online, your target audience is no longer local, but global. How can you make money by taking your business online? Here are a few ideas to get you started.

VLOGGING

You can make money by sharing your videos on YouTube. YouTube is a household name and a platform that attracts viewers from all over the world. For you as a business owner, this platform gives you the opportunity to share your professional experience and expertise with viewers across the globe. How cool is that? Provided you are good at what you do and what you share resonates with your audience, you have a good chance of making really good money through YouTube through ad revenue and sponsorships.

To make good money online, you must have a large audience. You need to have enough subscribers and viewers to make your channel attractive to advertisers. Four things are essential to achieve this target: consistency, high-quality videos, relevant content, and promotion. Here are a few ways to ensure you are hitting each one of these items as you are building your YouTube brand.

Consistency

You have to post videos consistently. For beginners, it might be a daunting task, especially if no one is watching your videos, but don't get discouraged. We've all been there!

How often should you post videos on YouTube? If you ask ten seasoned YouTubers, you might get five different answers. There isn't a hard and fast number for this, but the rule of thumb is at least once a week. Some people post as many as two to three videos each week. But be careful: for beginners especially, you need to devote time to producing videos that will resonate with your audience in terms of both content and quality. Do not sacrifice quality at the altar of quantity. It will backfire.

Quality

To grow and maintain an audience, you must upload high-quality videos that are relevant to your audience. This means investing time and energy into video production every week. You do not have to rob a bank to buy high-end equipment for recording and editing your videos. A good smartphone can do the trick for you if you can't afford a good camera at the beginning. However, if you are really serious about making money and you have the resources, why not invest in a high-quality camera right away? That was what I did the moment I decided that vlogging would be one of the ways I would promote my health, wellness, and healthy lifestyle messages. I have since been told by viewers that the quality of my videos is second to none.

Relevance

In addition to posting high quality videos consistently, you have to put your problem-solving skills to work. Look for problems within your niche or area of expertise that you can solve. Are there things people struggle with or would like to know more about within your field that you can show them how to solve?

For example, if you work in the nutrition industry, showing people how to eat an apple may not add value to the field. But helping people discover different ways to enjoy apples might get their attention. Videos titled "Healthy homemade applesauce" or "An easy way to slice apples at home" are examples of content that can captivate your audience.

For beginners, do not get caught in the trap of analysis paralysis. Don't waste too much time surfing the internet and reading books to figure out the type of content to post. Share your ideas, but make sure they resonate with your audience. It might take time to hit that sweet spot. From personal experience, sometimes you can't predict the video that will get a lot of views. As long as you are solving problems, you will get people to watch your videos and subscribe to your channel. It might take time, but it will happen.

Promotion! Promotion! Promotion!

You must promote your contents as if your life depends on it. If you are starting a brand-new business, it might be hard at first to convince people that you are worth following. If you already have an existing business and plan to take your expertise online and self-promote via YouTube, you probably already have a pre-existing following, which will work to your advantage. Inform your friends, neighbors and customers that you are live online. Leverage your customer base to promote your content. Use your existing social media platforms such as

Facebook, Twitter, Instagram or Pinterest to self-promote.

YOUTUBE REVENUE

Warning: Just because you posted hundreds of videos does not guarantee that you will make a dime within a month…or even a year. Think of your YouTube channel as a startup. It can take some startups up to five years to see a positive cash flow. Don't panic. While the end goal is to make money on YouTube, you should focus your attention on providing value to your audience. If you do that, and your audience likes what you share and trusts you, they will subscribe and watch more of your videos.

Once you build your audience and subscribers base, you should look for opportunities to monetize your YouTube channel. These opportunities include:

Ad Revenue

Ad revenue is the most commonly-known YouTube monetization option. If you have watched videos on YouTube, chances are pretty good you have seen ads pop up before the videos you want to watch. As much as I don't appreciate seeing some of those ads, there have been times I have clicked on ones I was interested in. Guess what? Any time you click on some of those ads, chances are that someone is getting paid.

Once you meet all the YouTube requirements – which include a certain number of required subscribers and a certain number of watch hours in a given year – you can apply for acceptance to the YouTube Partner Program. Once you get accepted, YouTube can choose to let ads on your videos. Anytime someone views/clicks on the ads that show up on your videos, you make money.[1] The more subscribers and views, the better your chance of making good money.

Product Promotion

Depending on the type of business you run or plan to start, you can make money by promoting any product you use to run your business. In fact, some companies pay influencers and businesses generously to promote their products on YouTube. As with ad revenue, the more subscribers and viewers you have, the higher the chances of making good money.

One caveat; you should always ensure you promote products that you can stand by, and preferably products that you have used in the past or currently use. If you promote a crappy product simply because you want to make money, you may lose your audience's trust. You want to avoid any negative publicity. If you are reviewing a product, be honest; let your audience know what you like and what you don't like about the product. Not only will you retain your audience's trust, but you will also position yourself as a reliable voice within your niche or industry.

Develop and Sell Your Own Products

As you perfect your craft within your niche, you can develop your own products, promote and sell them online. Your own YouTube channel is a great marketing platform. If you currently have existing products, you can leverage your online platforms to aggressively market and sell them. Note that I use the word "products" in a broader sense here; that term isn't limited to tangible products. Your services and knowledge can be considered products as well! Let's assume that you recently started a professional counseling business after vlogging about it for many years. That is a product that you can market and sell to your YouTube audience. If you are into natural beauty products and you develop a hair product, you can market it to your YouTube audience. The opportunities are endless. Get creative and start sharing with the world the wealth of information that you possess. Sooner or later, you could start monetizing that knowledge.

Before you dismiss vlogging and conclude that you are not good at making videos or showing your face on the internet, just know that everyone who took a leap of faith had similar doubts. The only difference is that they did not let their doubts keep them from doing vlogging. They did not allow their feeling of inadequacies to stop them. Neither did they allow self-doubt to stop them from venturing out. Before I launched my blog and, later, my YouTube channel, I would never allow a single photo of me on any social media platforms, let alone a video! I had to overcome my doubts, fears and excuses. The biggest challenge is taking that first step.

If you have an interested in a niche, do your due diligence to ensure that the market is not oversaturated. Then step out and start vlogging. However, if you are truly convinced that vlogging is not your thing, but you have some type of knowledge or interest in a particular niche that you want to take online, blogging might be an excellent choice for you. Let's take a look at blogging more closely.

START BLOGGING

I recently started blogging about health and wellness with a focus on holistic health. Although I'm still new to the blogging world, I have been working really hard to create multiple paths to make money from blogging. People suffer from too many preventable diseases, and I believe that creating an awareness about what causes diseases and natural ways to prevent diseases will ease the burden the healthcare industry currently faces. I'm not dedicating this book to promote my blog, but I wanted to share with you that if you have the passion for and knowledge about something, you can add value to your readers by blogging about your niche or field.

Blogging and vlogging go hand in hand. Similar to vlogging, blogging requires an audience – in this case, your readers. Like

YouTube, you have to post on a consistent basis if you ever want to build your base. You must publish high quality content that is relevant to your readers. Because I have already covered all these essentials in detail under vlogging, I will not describe them here. You can refer to that section for more detail. One more thing I would add is to make sure you retain readers – sometimes called subscribers – by promoting a newsletter or establishing a sign-up form on the side of your blog. That's how you ensure your readers keep coming back for more.

To make money while blogging, you will need a website. You can utilize several online platforms to promote your content, but all of that promotion should drive traffic back to your website. Doing so will increase the number of pageviews and site visitors, which is vital if you plan to monetize your blog. There are several ways to make money from your blog: ad revenue, affiliate marketing, digital products and sponsorships, to name a few.

Ad Revenue

Similar to YouTube ad revenue, you can earn revenue by placing ads on your website. If someone visits your website and clicks on the ads, you earn money. This is called cost per click (CPC). Alternatively, you can earn income through cost per thousand (CPM) - you get paid per 1,000 impressions or views regardless of if anyone clicks.[2] Most bloggers will agree that this is not the best way to earn money while blogging. However, it's one stream of income, and that's better than none. If you are new to the blogging world, ad revenue might be a good way to start earning a small amount of money each month.

Affiliate Marketing

With affiliate marketing, businesses compensate you for referring customers to their site. If you sign up for an affiliate program, you will get a tracking link that you can insert in your regular blog posts. If someone clicks on the link and makes a purchase, or signs up for a newsletter or subscription, you get paid a fixed amount or a previously-stipulated percentage of the sale. The Amazon affiliate marketing program is one of the more popular programs for beginner bloggers.

Online Courses and Digital Products

If you are a professional and are really good at what you do, you should consider yourself a subject matter expert in that area. Do not think that you need some type of special education or licensure to be qualified to teach people or help them learn how to solve problems that they already come to you for help. If you are already publishing great content online and people value the contents you put out there, you can take that information and package it in the form of an online course. This is a great way to earn good passive income (see chapter three). Any time someone pays and downloads the training material, you make money. The great thing about developing digital materials is that it does not cost too much money to put together. If you make that initial time investment to develop the course, any other major expense you might incur would be related to marketing your digital product.

Sponsored Ads

Sponsored ads are an amazing way to make money through your blog. But first, you have to grow your audience base, similar to how you must grow your YouTube subscribers or viewers. Sponsored ads work the same way as YouTube product promotions. For example, if you want to publish a post about starting a blog, you could weave into your post different products and services a new blogger would need in order to get a blog up and running. Any time someone clicks on the link and pays the blog hosting fee, for example, you get paid.

Physical products

If your audience is large enough where readers frequently come to your website for information, you can start an online store where you sell products within your blog niche that your site visitors will likely buy. If your blog niche is photography, for instance, you could develop and sell Lightroom presets or digital photography guides that are relevant to your readership.

The Internet and social media have created endless opportunities for those who want to venture out and become their own boss. Even if you currently own a small, thriving business, look into some of the ideas that I shared here and give them a try.

A personal or global recession has a way of crippling small businesses and wiping out their profits in a flash. The recent COVID-19 is another testament to this fact. Similarly, as a small business owner, if you suddenly get sick, you may not be able to run your business, but if you have taken your business online, you can continue to earn money while you are away. That is called passive income, my friend. We introduced Bobby at the beginning of this chapter. He found a way to turn his passion into a thriving business. Do likewise. Take action now. Take your tiny idea, passion, or talent and turn it into a business.

A FINAL WORD: THE BRICK AND MORTAR BUSINESS MODEL

In this chapter, I explained to you how to utilize the internet to launch an online business that is recession proof. If you believe your business model does not fit into what I described above, by all means, pursue your business the traditional way by operating out of a physical location. If you can't find a way to integrate into an online platform, by all means, run your business the traditional way and augment it with an online presence.

As you brainstorm your business ideas and model – whether that's building an online business, running a traditional business, or a mix of both – think about how a recession can impact your business. Regardless of how you choose to operate your business, find ways to build the ability to generate passive income into it. The good thing about passive income is that you can continue to make money even when you are not working. We will take a closer look at passive income in the next chapter.

Take a finance consultant for instance. How can you generate passive income through your finance consulting business? Teach people how to become a successful finance consultant. Develop an eBook about it or develop an online course. Are you a real estate investor? Why not develop an online course that shows people how to launch a real estate business that is guaranteed to generate constant positive cash flow? Any time someone downloads and buys your eBook or course, you earn income. There is no time limit. You can continue to generate a decent passive income for many years. People are desperate to try new things; if you develop relevant content that can solve people's problems and have the right platforms to promote your content, you can make good money. This is a proven business model that is constantly generating an inflow of passive income for many people.

Whatever you decide to do, do it now. Do not wait until tomorrow – it might be too late. If you build your business now, you are in a better position to weather the storm of recession, survive it and even thrive. Recessions have ways of punishing people who fail to plan and prepare in advance. It's high time you became your own boss.

Starting your own business is important; equally important is deciding the form of business structure that will suit your business need.

FORMS OF BUSINESS ORGANIZATIONS

Now that you have understood different ways to become your own boss, let us delve into another important aspect of starting a business: business structure. From accounting standpoint, once you decide to start a business, regardless of the type, your business is considered a distinct or separate entity from you. This means that all your business activities must be kept separate from your personal financial transactions. You cannot commingle your business finances with your personal finances. For instance, if you own a graphic design business and you bought a laptop solely for personal use, you cannot consider the cost of the laptop a business expense. However, if you use the same laptop for both personal and business activities, you can deduct a portion of the cost of the laptop as a business expense on your tax returns.

Taxes are another important reason why you should keep your business transactions separate from personal transactions. Business expenses are tax deductible but personal expenses are not. Moreover, you are required to report all your business income when you file your tax returns. Therefore, in order to accurately report your expenses and income, you should keep your business transactions separate from personal transactions.

There are four common forms of business organization that most startups and small owners choose: sole proprietorship, limited liability company, partnership, and corporation I will explain key characteristics of each to enable you to determine the best form of business that suits your business needs. Because the accounting and legal side of being a business owner can be complex, it is crucial that you talk to a financial advisor, lawyer or accountant to ensure that you not only set up your business correctly, but also follow the accounting rules when recording financial activities and paying taxes.

SOLE PROPRIETORSHIP

A sole proprietorship is a form of business that is owned by a single person and usually managed by the same person. Over 25 million people operate their businesses as sole proprietors, and 73% of all businesses in the U.S. are sole proprietorships, making it the most common type of business organization in the United States.[3] Although a sole proprietor owns and sometimes manages the business by himself or herself, the business is still considered distinct from the owner, for accounting purposes. From the legal standpoint, however, the sole proprietor is not considered a separate legal entity.[4] The owner and the business are one and the same.

Still, the owner must maintain a separate financial activity of the business such as the cost of operating the business and the income generated from selling products or services. For instance, a sole proprietor should not record personal expenses such as a car note or a monthly cell phone payment as business expenses.

BENEFITS OF A SOLE PROPRIETORSHIP

Starting a sole proprietorship business has some advantages. First, the owner has full control and ownership over his or her business. Making decisions on how to operate the business can be done faster, unlike the other forms of business, where decision making process can be prolonged.

Second, a single owner keeps all the profit from running the business. The owner does not share the business profit with other partners or owners, unlike limited liability companies or corporations.

Third, a sole proprietorship is the easiest form of business organization to start. There are no complicated paper filings, and there are no stringent requirements to meet. To exist as a sole proprietor, there is no requirement to register your business with the state; you are automatically considered a sole proprietor once you start doing a business.

However, you may be required to obtain state or local licenses and permits in order to legitimize your business and be in compliance with local business regulations. If you choose a business name other than your personal name, you may be required to register with the state. For instance, if your name is John Smith, but your business name is Smith Carpet Cleaning, some states will require you to register your business, often called fictitious name.[5] Check the state where you live to ensure that there are no additional filing requirements before starting your business.

Fourth, unlike a corporation, a sole proprietorship business does not pay corporate taxes. A sole proprietor pays taxes on the business income only, which he or she reports on the personal income tax. The business income and expenses are reported on Schedule C, which flows into Form 1040. But you will have to pay self-employment taxes to account for contributions to Medicare and Social Security. This is reported on Schedule SE.

DRAWBACKS TO SOLE PROPRIETORSHIP

There are few downsides to a sole proprietorship that you should be aware of. First, your ability to raise capital in order to grow and expand your business is limited. You can't raise capital by issuing shares or selling interest in your business. This is one benefit that corporations and limited liability companies enjoy. Essentially, a sole proprietor is limited to borrowing money from friends and family or using personal money to grow his or her business. Unfortunately, it is challenging to attract investors or get a substantial loan or line of credit from lending institutions if you are a sole proprietor.

Secondly, the single owner is personally liable for the business' debts and liabilities. If you are unable to meet your business obligations or pay your creditors, they can bring lawsuits against you and you may be required to use your personal assets such as home and bank accounts to satisfy your business obligations.

Thirdly, just as the owner enjoys 100% of the business profits, he or she absorbs all the business losses.

Fourthly, a sole proprietorship usually does not survive the incapability or death of the owner. In other words, the business folds once the owner is dead or is incapable of managing the business due to illness, old age or other factors.

Most small businesses start as sole proprietorship but later change to other forms of business to accommodate the business growth. So, if you are unsure of the business structure to form, sole proprietorship might be a good place to start, but you have to weigh the costs (no assets protection and minimal tax benefits) against the benefits. You can always change to an LLC or Corporation as your business expands.

LIMITED LIABILITY COMPANY (LLC)

A limited liability company is a form of business organization wherein owners (also known as members) are not personally liable for the company's debts or liabilities. Forming a limited liability company is less complex than forming a corporation. However, you may be required to register with your state, file articles of organization and operating agreement, and follow certain state regulations. Because an LLC is allowed by state statute, you should check with your state if this is the business structure that suits your business need.[6] To avoid making mistakes that could put you in a legal jeopardy, I recommend that you work with a qualified CPA or an attorney if you decide to incorporate your business as an LLC.

Additionally, instead of a regular limited liability company, you can create a single-member LLC. A single-member LLC shares similar characteristics of regular LLC, except that is owned by a single owner.

An LLC is the preferred form of business organization to start if you do not want to be held personally liable for your company's debts or lawsuits and you do not want to undergo the rigorous process of forming a corporation. Members of an LLC are not obligated to use their personal money to pay the business' debts; neither are they at risk of losing their personal assets to settle a lawsuit against the business.[7]

Similar to a sole proprietorship, an LLC is not subject to double taxation. The owners do not pay taxes on the business income. Instead, they report business income and expenses on their personal tax returns. Alternatively, an LLC can elect to be treated as a corporation for tax purposes. This means that an LLC must follow the filing requirements and tax laws that govern a corporation.[8]

PARTNERSHIP

A partnership is a business structure formed by two or more partners. A partnership shares several characteristics of an LLC, such as limited liability protection and tax benefits. In some cases, no formal agreement is required to form a partnership. Once two or more individuals engage in a business activity with the intention of making a profit, it is considered a partnership.

However, you should not operate a partnership without a formal partnership agreement. It will save you unnecessary disputes in the future. Everyone's responsibilities, obligations, and ownership stake in the business should be enshrined in the partnership agreement. To receive the personal liability protection and tax advantages, you should legitimize your partnership by registering with your state and filing all the required documents, including an Article of Partnership. You can form a general partnership, limited partnership or limited liability partnership.

A general partnership does not provide owners limited liable protection.[9] This mean the owners can be held liable for the partnership's debts, and be required to settle partnership's debts and lawsuits with their personal assets. Without the liability protection, a general partnership is a risky business structure to form. A better option is a limited partnership or a limited liability partnership.

In a limited partnership, partners enjoy limited liability protection. However, the general partner, who normally engages in daily operation of the business, assumes the unlimited liability of the partnership. In other words, the general partner can be held responsible for the partnership's obligations and liabilities. As a result of the unlimited liability protection, the general partner may get a larger share of the partnership.[10] Also, the general partner may exercise more authority than the other partners and make business decisions without the consent of the other partners.[11] A limited liability partnership is similar to limited partnership, except that all partners are not personally liable for the debts and liabilities of the partnership.

Also, limited partnership and limited liability partnership businesses are not subject to double taxation. Instead, the business earnings pass through to partners, who report the income and losses on their personal tax returns and pay taxes on their share of the business earnings. It is advisable to check with your state's requirements and work with a reputable attorney or a CPA.

CORPORATION

A corporation is a form of business organization that is owned by shareholders (also called stockholders). This is the most complex of the three forms of business organizations. To incorporate a business as a corporation, you are required to register with your state and be governed under stringent state laws.[12]

Similar to an LLC, a corporation is a distinct legal business entity. Therefore, shareholders are not personally liable for the company's debts or liabilities.

Another benefit of a corporation is the ability to raise capital. In exchange for cash or other assets, a corporation can issue shares, which represent the ownership interest in the business. Because a corporation can have unlimited number of owners, it can issue shares to unlimited number of investors and raise sufficient capital to expand its business. Other than issuing shares, a corporation can raise capital by issuing debt securities such as bonds, commercial paper, and certificate of deposit (CD).

In addition, since a corporation is considered a legal business entity distinct from the owners, the business can exist in perpetuity; the death of shareholders does not lead to the dissolution of the business.[13]

One major downside of a corporation is that the owners (shareholders) pay taxes twice. This is called double taxation. First, a corporation pays taxes on its profit. Second, shareholders pay taxes when they receive dividends from the business. Unlike an LLC or a sole proprietorship where owners deduct business losses on their personal tax returns, shareholders are not allowed to deduct losses of the corporation on their tax returns.[14]

A corporation is subject to more oversight and regulations by both state and federal governments. This means that the business must file Articles of Incorporation, bylaws, quarterly and annual reports as well as other complicated tax filings and regulatory reporting.[15] Also, the cost of filing these reports can be high.

Another form of a corporation to consider is S corporation. Essentially, an S corporation is similar to a corporation (or C corporation) that I described above. However, this business structure differs from a corporation in few ways. An S corporation is not subject to double taxation. Instead, shareholders report the income and losses of the business on their personal tax returns. An S corporation cannot be a foreign corporation; it must be a domestic corporation. It must not have more than 100 shareholders, can only issue one class of common stock, and can only have U.S. citizens and permanent residents as shareholders.[16]

CHAPTER 3

PASSIVE INCOME NOW

"If you don't find a way to make money while you sleep, you will work until you die." –Warren Buffet.

Josh was the guy anyone would love to meet. He brightened everyone's day with humor and was a great encourager. Friends and family came to him for advice and words of wisdom whenever they went through difficult times.

He was a truck driver and had a hectic schedule, but those long hours on the road never stopped him from smiling at people, and spending time with his wife Mia and daughter Olivia. Barbecuing was his thing. Anytime he was off on a weekend, Josh would grill some burgers, chicken, corn, and vegetables. He would invite his neighbors and friends to join him. They would talk about football all night long.

Troubles can knock on the door unannounced, and Josh was not immune from that. On April 14, 2011, Josh was driving along the I-20 from Dallas, Texas to Atlanta, Georgia when tragedy struck. It was raining and it was dark. Another 18-wheeler truck driver lost control of his truck due to poor vision and slippery roads, veered off the road and hit Josh's truck on the driver's side. Both trucks fell into a ditch.

Before the state troopers, firefighters and ambulances arrived on the scene, Josh's truck had caught fire with him trapped inside. Firefighters worked hard and fast to put out the fire and first responders swung into action to pull Josh and the other driver from their trucks.

Sadly, by the time the other driver was pulled out of his truck, he had passed away from severe injury he sustained on his head. Josh survived the accident, but his life was never the same again. He sustained multiple injuries on his legs and back. Doctors worked so hard to repair the broken bones, unfortunately, they were only able to save one of Josh's legs. His right leg was amputated.

Once Josh began to heal, the doctor broke the bad news to him. "You will never be able to drive again." At first, he was in denial, but as days turned into weeks and weeks turned into months, the reality of his predicament began to settle in. Josh sank into depression. He became very discouraged. Sometimes, he would not leave his house for weeks. Sometimes he skipped the therapy sessions. The smile that once radiated from Josh's face had faded. All you could see was gloom and despair.

Gradually, Josh began to withdraw from this family, his friends, and his society. He would go for days without saying a word to his wife and daughter. Mia was very supportive, but she struggled to help Josh regain his joy and happiness. Many days, Olivia would cry herself to sleep because Daddy wouldn't talk to her and Mommy.

One morning, Mia woke up and did not see Josh in the bed. She yelled his name, hoping that he was in the bathroom, but she got no response. She hurried down the stairs, and saw a note on a paper towel on the living room table: "I'm sorry. Couldn't bear the pain anymore. I love you." Josh took his own life on November 5, 2011 at the age of 41. Those last words scribbled on a paper towel have haunted Mia for many years. Josh's death created untold financial hardships for Mia and Olivia because Josh was the sole provider for the family. Mia was forced to sell their house and move to a 2-bedroom apartment. Seven months after the death of her husband, Mia struggled to find a steady job to support her family financial needs. Fortunately, Josh invested in several blue-chip stocks, and he had a join ownership with Mia. The passive income in form of cash dividends from the various stock investments helped alleviate Mia's financial burdens. She used the money to take care of herself and Olivia while she searched for a reliable job.

The death of her Daddy created emotional pain for Olivia. It got so bad that Olivia's Mommy had to take her to a child counsellor who assisted her to deal with the sadness and grief of losing her Daddy.

In its simplest form, passive income is income that you earn after an initial investment, and continue to earn money from the investment without making substantial and continuous financial or time commitments. After the initial investment of time or money, little to no time or work should be expensed to earn the passive income. Otherwise it's clearly not considered passive income.

Let's assume that last year you spent 30 hours a week to create an eBook and earned $1,000. Five months later, you spent another 30 hours creating a second eBook and earned another $1500. This is not a passive income because it took you almost the same time and effort to generate the same amount of money. On the other hand, pretend that you spent 100 hours last year to develop an eBook, spent $500 to market it, and earned $10,000 income. A year later, you invested just 5 hours and spent $500 to promote that same eBook, generated $4,000, and continue to generate income in subsequent years without any extra promotion. This is considered passive income. Passive income is one of the most powerful and effective tools that you should have in your recession preparation and readiness toolbox.

WHY PASSIVE INCOME NOW?

If you think of passive income as the money that you make while you are asleep, then you can understand why having some type of passive income now is crucial before recession rears its ugly head. The biggest pressure most people deal with is financial pressure. Personal finance is one area that gets hit the most during recession. Knowing that your stream of income won't run dry even in the nastiest of recessions can give you some level of comfort and peace of mind. Mia would not have sustained her family during the darkest time of her life had she not received the passive income from her husband's investments. Just remember that passive income alone might not be enough to survive and thrive during a personal financial crisis. It's a great safety net, but don't assume that it will be enough to sustain you.

WAYS TO EARN PASSIVE INCOME

There are multiple ways to earn passive income, but I'm going to focus on five different ways. There are a lot more out there; a quick search online will give you few other options and ideas.

Books

Writing and publishing books can be a daunting task, but it comes with a generous financial reward. A few years ago, I edited and published an accounting textbook that launched nationwide. I used the textbook to teach financial and managerial accounting at a university, and other accounting colleagues taught with the textbook, too. I spent hundreds of hours on that project. Once the textbook was published, my work was done. I did not spend any more time on the textbook, except when I published another edition. Any time someone purchased the textbook, my publisher paid me royalties. I still receive royalties from time to time, even though it's been many years since I published the book. With self-publishing almost surpassing traditional publishing, the opportunity to publish a book is now wide open.

If you choose to publish traditionally, the process of getting your book published can be long, and the publisher may require you to change or modify some of the original content of your book or you may be turned away. Additionally, because the publisher does the majority of publishing work for you, they get to keep a bigger share of the book's proceeds. If you work with good publishers, they can help ensure that your book gets a lot of visibility. This may include distributing your book to multiple bookstores, and promoting your book to a wider audience.

If you choose the self-publishing route – like I did for this book – you have autonomy. However, this means you are responsible for everything that goes into publishing. This includes formatting, cover design, publishing and promotion. The good news is that you can make more money from books as a self-published author than you can through a traditional publisher. And just because you choose to self-publish does not mean that you do all the work. You can work with individuals or a self-publishing company to assist in the process.

You can decide to publish your book in different formats such as paperback, eBook, or audiobook. If you have a great idea that you can turn into a book but you are concerned that the information is not big enough to be published in paperback, an eBook can be an excellent option for you. Additionally, the process of self-publishing eBooks costs less money than the cost publishing a paperback, since you don't have to pay for printing and distribution expenses.

Another alternative that is growing in popularity is audio-books. With an audio book, you or someone that you pay records an audio version of your written book. Regardless of the publishing method you choose – self-publishing or traditional publishing – and the format that you prefer – paperback, eBook, or audiobook – publishing a book is a sure way to earn passive income.

Real Estate

Investing in real estate could be a lucrative source of passive income. If you want to earn passive income from real estate, then you have to invest in rental properties. From a passive income standpoint, as long as your cash inflow from the rental property is greater than cash outflow, you are guaranteed to earn passive income. By purchasing and renting properties through a real estate agent, online listings or short-term rental websites like Airbnb, you can maintain a steady flow of income.

For the nuances and other intricate details about real estate, I highly recommend that you talk to a real estate specialist. Keep in mind that a global or national recession can adversely affect real estate. Real estate was one of the major sectors of the U.S. economy that suffered greatly during the Great Recession. If people are losing jobs and businesses are closing, chances are that you might have a hard time collecting your rent. If you decide to get into real estate, you should invest some time and resources and learn about the business. Look up local classes in your area or invest in some college courses that can give you a solid foundation of knowledge.

Songs or Movies

If you have the gift of writing, singing or media and entertainment production, why not invest heavily in developing that talent? You get paid royalties any time someone buys or downloads your products. For instance, copyright on songs can last up to 70 years after the death of the song writer. One can continue to earn passive income even after death.

Self-Developed Online Courses

Similar to books, if you develop an online course, you will continue to earn passive income as long as someone buys the course. There is no time limit.

What are you good at? Do you have a special interest in something that you are knowledgeable about? Why not develop a course and help solve people's problems? Provided your course is relevant and you have the right platforms to market it, you will earn a decent passive income.

Here are some example topics you can turn into an online course and earn some passive income:

- DIY guides (gardening, breadmaking, pottery, or any other hands-on skill)
- Language learning
- Soft skills (music, handcrafts, simple repairs)

I hope that these examples can spark an idea. Do your research. What does your niche or market need? What expertise can you provide? Turn that knowledge into an online course and watch the profits flow.

Dividends

Cash dividends are a great way to earn passive income. If you invest in a company's stock, you're guaranteed to get a cut anytime the company declares and pays dividends. Depending on how many shares you own, you could receive generous cash dividends.

The good thing about dividends is that as long as the company continues to exist, perform well, and pay dividends, you are guaranteed to get paid. However, there are downsides to investing in any portfolio that is tied to market performance. Typically, companies' stocks tend to nosedive during recessions. If a recession lasts for a long period of time, it means that your likelihood of getting cash dividends when you need it the most might be slim. This is another reason why you should diversify your portfolio.

If you are an investing novice, talk to a financial advisor or your banker. Work with experts to create a portfolio that is as recession-proof as possible. While no one can predict the future, there are trends investors rely on to ensure their client's investments and dividends remain safe even during uncertain times.

Beside these five ways to earn passive income that I listed above, there are other ways to earn passive income. They include affiliate marketing, YouTube ads, developing an app or program, and a high yield account. Depending on your interest, a quick online search will show you various ways to earn passive income.

The key is to plan, prepare, and start now. Don't procrastinate. Invest in something that will generate passive income for you. Having a reliable and consistent inflow of passive income during recession can help alleviate some of your financial woes.

CHAPTER 4

CREATE A SIDE HUSTLE NOW

"Good things happen to those who hustle." –Anais Nin.

Cindy was a single mother of three - two boys and a girl, ages seven, five and two. She was well acquainted with crisis; anytime she attempted to pick her life up, something else knocked her down.

After the birth of her second child, Cindy suffered from severe depression that almost destroyed her life. It got so bad that she had to quit her administrative assistant job, and it took multiple months of counseling to get her back on her feet. She considered taking her own life on several occasions, but with the help of her health coach and counselor, Cindy recovered and regained her optimal weight by shedding 114 pounds in just six months.

Cindy was excited to return to work. A close friend of hers helped her secure another administrative assistant job at a growing company that specialized in cleaning brand new homes and commercial buildings. To say she was excited was an understatement. Just the opportunity to leave the house brought so much joy in her life. Sadly, that didn't last long.

Three years, two months and five days after she fully recovered from depression, her life came tumbling down again. In summer of 2004, Cindy was pregnant with her third child. One day, about five weeks before she was due, she got a call that her husband had an accident at his construction site. Minutes after she arrived at the hospital, her husband passed away from the injury he sustained.

Cindy was inconsolable. She sunk into depression again, but with the help of family members, friends and professional counselors, she slowly, but progressively, improved. To support her family and her newborn baby, Cindy often worked two to three side hustle jobs. Life became really hard for her and her family. Ensuring that her three children ate well and that bills were paid on time became a big challenge.

In December 2007, Cindy found herself again fighting for her life and that of her family. As everybody was busy preparing for Christmas, Cindy was fighting to keep her lights on and feed herself and her kids after losing her two side hustle jobs in the span of three weeks. Her saving grace was that, fortunately, she had retained her $35,000 a year administrative assistant job. But bills were still piling up, and there were no jobs in sight.

On July 10, 2008, Cindy's home was foreclosed and she was forced to become homeless. She and her kids were in and out of shelters for several months, and at the same time, she was battling depression. It became so bad that she had to check into a mental institution for a few months. At that point, it became obvious that she could no longer care for her kids while fighting for her life. On November 17, 2008, Cindy formally gave a temporary guardianship of her kids to her mother.

As she gradually recovered from depression, Cindy got two side hustle jobs; she worked as a nanny during the day and a waitress in the evening. She saved enough money and moved into a 2-bed room apartment. Nine months after living without her kids, Cindy finally reunited with her kids.

A side hustle, as the name suggests, is an additional means of supplementing one's income. A side hustle can be a part-time job or jobs outside of one's regular full-time job. Anyone can have a side job, but most people who hustle on the side may already struggle with their finances. Therefore, they need additional income to supplement their income from full-time jobs. On the other hand, some people who have side jobs may be financially stable. They may create a side hustle because they have a passion for that particular profession or field, but without their regular jobs, they cannot sustain themselves financially. For that reason, they need full-time jobs to pay the bills while they continue to pursue their passion. Also, some people may choose to pursue a side job with the intention of making it a full-time job or business later in the future. In the meantime, they need a full-time job that will provide them with the income that they need to take care of personal and family financial responsibilities.

WHY A SIDE HUSTLE IS GOOD

A side hustle creates another stream of income for you. It could become a life saver when recession strikes. Because a recession does not discriminate based on income or socioeconomic status, it is imperative that everyone be prepared and as financially stable as possible.

Think about the Great Recession or the COVID-19 pandemic. Millions of people lost their jobs during these crises. If your only source of income is your full-time job and you lose it, you are more likely to experience personal financial crisis than someone who retains their side job during the crisis or someone who has a side hustle job.

While you would ideally craft your side hustle around things you are passionate and knowledgeable about, make sure your side hustle will also sustain you in a recession. If a recession strikes, are you at risk of losing both your full-time job and your side hustle job? If you have no preference in terms of a side hustle you want to pursue, then your options are much broader than someone who has preferences. Before Cindy lost her home, she had two side hustle jobs that were not recession-proof. Obviously, losing your major sources of income simultaneously can create serious financial burdens. Therefore, you must be strategic about choosing your side hustle.

MAKE YOUR SIDE HUSTLE A FULL-TIME GIG

You can start a side hustle with the intention of making it a full-time business. Let's say you work in the technology sector but you have a passion for fitness. You typically go to the gym five times a week and you love to talk to people about your fitness experience. You could get a side job at a fitness center now and pick a schedule that works for you. While you're there, learn the business side of fitness. Learn how to run a successful business. Bring customers to the company and become their personal trainer. You not only will bring in additional income, but also gain valuable experience that could prove beneficial whenever you decide to launch your own fitness business. In line with this example, virtual fitness coaching (or the side hustle of your choice) is another alternative if you don't want to be bound by a physical location. This is just one example of how you can turn a side hustle into a full-time business. You can apply this example to any side hustle job that has the potential to become a full-time business.

Take a trucking business, for example. You rent a truck and deliver items to people's homes or businesses maybe on weekends and/or after your regular job. This can be a good side hustle job that can fetch you some reasonable income. With time, you can turn your side hustle into a business that pays more than your regular job. Similar to fitness training examples, you have to dedicate time to learn the business and the industry (including training, licensing, and regulatory requirements) before venturing into it. Otherwise, you may end up building sometime that will not last, sustain you in the future, or survive a recession. When creativity meets planning and preparation, success is all but guaranteed. I can give you countless examples to spur some thoughts, but the model works the same.

SIDE HUSTLE AS A SAVING/INVESTMENT STRATEGY

If your current job takes care of your financial needs, you can still get a side job now and channel all the income toward saving and investing. I believe this strategy is smart, especially if you work in an industry that gets hit the most during recessions. If your industry suffers massively during the recession, the risk of losing your job is high. Your side hustle can become your rainy-day fund. You can save a portion of your income from side hustle and invest the rest in anything from short-term to long-term investments.

If a side hustle job is a means to meet your day-to-day or month-to-month financial needs, you might want to think about other ways to increase your income. Do you need a different job that pays you more money? Do you need to improve your skills by going back to school or taking a certificate program specific to your field? Do you need to explore other career options? Or do you need to start your own business? If you need multiple jobs to take care of your financial obligations, this could be an ominous sign that you may not survive the financial storm if you were to experience any recession - personal or otherwise. Now is the right time to reevaluate your skillset, talents, and lifestyle.

SIDE HUSTLES TO CONSIDER

The table below will show you some examples of side hustle jobs out there. There are more side hustle jobs than I listed here. The list will give you an idea of different types of side hustle jobs in case you are not familiar with them. You can do your own research for more side hustle jobs. You can engage in any of these jobs, provided your regular jobs allows you to do so.[1]

Amazon driver	Lyft driver	Uber driver	Grocery delivery	Pizza delivery
Hair stylist	Barber	Babysitter	Nanny	Fitness trainer
Dog trainer	Dog walker	Waiter/ waitress	Bartender	Music instructor
Health coach	Kids' league coach	Small league referee	House sitter	Dance instructor
Tutor	Tour guide	Decorator	Swimming instructor	Mystery shopper
Virtual assistant	Aerobics instructor	Modeling	DJ	Freelancer

As you can see, most of these side hustles are low-paying. That's why they are called side hustles. You hustle on the side to earn a little extra money to supplement your income from your full-time job. Except when you have a side hustle job for the reasons I shared above, side hustle jobs might not be the best way to sustain yourself financially. If you have extra time on hand, why not invest it on something that can generate you passive income for a very long time (chapter 3)? Or start your own business (chapter 2) such as blogging/vlogging, ecommerce business, to name a few? Some of these business ventures can start as side hustles and then mature into full blown business. If that's your goal, then it will make sense to pursue a side hustle job. There are few issues with side hustles that you should be aware of.

ISSUES WITH SIDE HUSTLE

If you already have a full-time job, chances are that your schedule is very demanding. Adding an additional side hustle may come at the expense of personal or family time. Moreover, you may experience burnout due to excessive hours you have to put in each day. Your health might tank, too. These are some factors that you must consider if you decide to look for a side hustle job. This is why, as I already mentioned, your ultimate goal should be to turn your side hustle into a self-sustaining business. Alternatively, use your side hustle as a saving or investment strategy.

There are better ways to augment your income if your full-time job does not cover all your financial needs. If, for whatever reason, you can't pursue other ways to increase your income, having a side job that does not interfere with your regular full-time job or quality of life is better than nothing. Always ensure that you do not run into problems with your full-time employer. Don't risk losing your full-time job simply because you needed a little extra cash to supplement your regular income. If you can navigate some of these hurdles well, then you should consider a side hustle.

CHAPTER 5

RESIZE NOW

"My riches consist not in extent of my possessions but in the fewness of my wants." –Joseph Brotherton.

Ted and Kate exchanged their marriage vows on the beautiful island of St. Lucia in the fall of 2002. Ted and Kate were college sweethearts who graduated one year before they got married. Both couples worked in the airline industry; Ted was an internal auditor and Kate was a software engineer. They both liked their jobs and they loved each other.

In 2005, Kate became pregnant and later that year, she gave birth to a handsome baby boy Drew. Drew was everything to Kate and Ted. Two months after Drew was born, Ted and Kate bought a brand-new home in the suburbs of Newark, New Jersey. Both couples liked traveling. In just two and half years, they had visited nine countries. To maintain their adventurous lifestyles, they spent a substantial amount of money traveling, and consequently, accumulated some debts.

Then came the turn of events in both couples' lives that shook the very core of their relationship.

It was a fateful summer of 2008 that Kate would never forget. She had taken a day off from work and was playing with

Drew in the front yard when Ted pulled into the driveway. He did not look very cheerful, although he managed to smile and kiss both Kate and Drew before heading inside the house. Kate hurriedly took Drew inside the house, fed him dinner, and put him to bed. Kate was anxious to know what was going on with Ted, because he did not join them at the family dinner table.

They sat in the sunroom, and Ted broke the bad news to Kate. He lost his job. Recession had impacted the airline industry so badly that thousands of people were laid off. Ted was devastated. Kate tried to encourage him, but couldn't.

Other than a few colleagues at work and some neighbors he had occasional chats and drinks with, Ted did not have a good support network. He turned to alcohol to soothe the emotional pain of losing his job and not being able to find another. His alcohol problem began to create issues between him and Kate. Numerous times, Kate encouraged Ted to get help, but he refused. Fortunately, Kate's job was not affected, but things began to get tough financially. Four months after losing his job, Ted became hopeless. The only place he found tenuous comfort was in alcohol. The problem got so bad that Ted began to verbally abuse Kate and Drew.

Kate feared for her life and that of her son. One late evening after Ted had drunk himself to stupor, Kate secretly took Drew and fled to her parents' house. Ted refused to accept help even after Kate arranged for him to see a counsellor. After multiple attempts to help her husband – her college sweetheart, and the love of her life – Kate decided to end her marriage. In March 2009, Kate officially filed for a divorce.

I recall reading multiple mainstream news articles in January of 2020 as some companies released their earnings. Some of the news media dubbed the earnings as the best performance of all time. You would think that these companies would increase their employees' bonuses and salaries. Businesses cut back on spending for various reason. But one of the major reasons is to prepare for a potential financial meltdown. Just like businesses, you must prepare for an anticipated or unexpected crisis by managing your expenses well. Resize willfully now to avoid downsizing forcibly when recession strikes.

You don't have to wait until you experience a personal financial meltdown before you start to trim your expenses. Businesses do this as a strategic move to weather any impending financial storms. Expense management does not necessarily mean living like a pauper just because you do not want to get caught in a financial storm. It means finding areas where you can cut back on spending. It means stepping back and thoroughly reviewing your finances and spending to determine certain lifestyles that you may not be able to sustain if recession hits.

Would you rather cut back now on certain exorbitant lifestyles that you can't sustain in a time of personal financial crisis, or be forced to do it when faced with a sudden financial firestorm? Those who fail to make expense management a key strategy to weather any adverse effect of recessions are punished severely; they suffer the most and they suffer the longest.

WHY YOU SHOULD RESIZE NOW

The old saying, "cut your coat according to your size" perfectly paints the picture of what resizing represents. From an expense perspective, most people walk around with oversized coats, meaning that they live beyond their means. You have to intentionally live within your means if you ever want to survive recession. Most recessions bring about financial hardships. Income tends to shrink, but expenses don't. You still have to pay your mortgage or rent, car loans, credit card debts, student loans, utilities, medical bills and phone bills. If you fail to pay any of these debts, you could face severe consequences and harm your credit score.

REVISIT YOUR LIFESTYLE

To adequately revisit and resize your lifestyle, you need to ask yourself some life-changing questions:

- Am I currently living above my means?
- Am I overspending?
- Are there areas that I can cut back spending and still enjoy my normal lifestyle?
- Do I have enough savings to absorb any unexpected expenses?

Obviously, the best option is always to increase your income and not cut expenses, particularly those expenses that are essential to life and happiness. For instance, a vacation is a fun way to enjoy life, and a decent home and a nice car are not bad either. However, if your financial state changes suddenly and you are forced to cut back on one of these areas – or other areas that you deem important – your wellbeing and happiness may suffer. Cutting certain expenses is a good practice, but increasing your income is a better option. That's why I devoted the three chapters in this book to show you different ways you can increase your income.

Regardless of your level of income, revising your lifestyles and spending habits are good expense management strategies you should employ from time to time. Never confuse needs with wants. Needs are essential for life's sustenance, but wants are not. If you can't meet your needs during recession, your personal wellbeing may be affected negatively. If you can't meet your wants, you may be mildly inconvenienced, but you will live.

Many years ago, my wife and I were paying more than $150 in monthly phone bills for our two phones. Mind you that this was one of the cheapest data plans the phone company offered at the time. We did not have a lot of money, so we had to slash the data twice. The first time, our bill came down to around $120. The second time, the bill came down to around $100. The issue? We did not have enough data and some months, we went over our limit and ended paying more. Not wise.

I did some research, and found another company that offered more data, charged less, and had similar quality of service. We switched to the new service provider and paid around $58 each month. We have been with the same phone company for about four years now. If we had continued to pay the original $150 before we switched to the new company, we would not have been saving $92 each month. If you multiply the number by 12, that would be $1,104 in savings each year. If you take it one step further and multiply the yearly savings by the four years that we have been with the new company, we would have saved $4,416 in just four years. That is a lot of money, at least to some people.

I hope you get the picture. Revisit your spending and look for ways to cut back expenses.

BUDGET NOW

Some people think that "budgeting" is an overused word. That might be true, but it is an effective way to manage your spending. If you budget and follow your budget strictly, you will find areas that you may be overspending and may be able to cut down on impulsive spending. Budgeting also gives you a pictorial view of your income and expenses. Depending on how you budget - spreadsheet, pen and paper, or advanced application - you are able to see your month-to-month, quarter-to-quarter or even year-to-year income and expenditures. If you are not sure how to start, you can start with a monthly budget. If you need to change to quarterly or annually, you can do so later on.

Personally, I believe that a monthly budget is the most

realistic, since that is how most people pay their recurring expenses such as mortgage, insurance and utilities. I prepare my family budget on a monthly basis. But you can adjust to whatever works for you. The end goal is to have a working budget.

If you have not been budgeting or you don't know how to start, you can search online for budget templates. Most of them have built-in formulas; you just plug in your numbers. Budgeting will help you stay organized and champion a saving mindset.

INCREASE YOUR NET WORTH

Once you revisit your spending habits and start to budget regularly, the next step is to look for opportunities to increase your net worth. Your net worth is simply the difference between what you own and what you owe, your assets and your liabilities. You want your net worth to continue to trend up each year. As you revisit your spending habits on a regular basis and cut down on spending, you should redirect the extra savings towards increasing your assets. This is a good financial habit to practice at least once a year.

If you see that your net worth is trending downward, it's time to revisit your spending. Did you increase your debt? Are you living above your means? Are you making the right investments and/or are your investments not appreciating? You will not be able to answer these questions if you do not take inventory of your net worth at least annually.

INCREASE YOUR INVESTMENTS

Adults in the United States spend about $18,000 a year on needless items or things they can do without.[1] Ironically, almost 70% of Americans have less than $1,000 in their savings accounts.[2] Do you see the problem? People are over-spending themselves into empty bank accounts.

Most people think that they need higher-paying jobs in order to save and invest. While that is true in some cases, you can save and invest simply by slashing unnecessary expenses. It's almost impossible to invest if you do not save; if you fail to invest, it's almost certain that you will remain in financial bondage for a good part of your life. Harsh but true.

Let's take the above scenario for example. Imagine investing a third of $18,000 (or $6,000) each year in some type of ordinary annuity that yields about 5% return. Let's further assume that you are 35 years old and you continue to invest the same amount until the age of 60. If you do a simple calculation by using a financial calculator or Excel, you will see you would have accumulated about $286,362.59 by the time you turn 60. That's the power of compounding.

Of course, this is just a simple example that assumes that you would continue to earn the same return on your investment each year. Even if you choose not to invest, but save $6,000 each year for the same duration of time, you will have $150,000 in your savings account. Of course, that would not be a smart thing to do. But you can see from the above example that no additional salary or income was required. It's just resizing and channeling the extra savings toward investments.

If you are not familiar with how investment in securities work, you should talk to an investment advisor to guide you in making those decisions. It is always important to diversify your portfolios. If your investment is tied to market performance, you should know your risk appetite and ensure that you are getting a return on your investment. Do not keep all your eggs in one basket.

IMPROVE YOUR CREDIT SCORE

This will be more relevant to someone who has too much

debt or is close to maxing out on a credit card. If you have a lot of debt and are struggling to pay it off, chances are that your credit score will be impacted negatively.

It's no-brainer that the higher your credit usage, the lower your credit score. If you miss your payments or any of your accounts become delinquent, you may be at risk of having derogatory remarks on your credit report. This is the reason why you should implement good expense management, especially if you are behind on your debts or are paying high interest. By reviewing your spending habits and reducing your expenses where necessary, you can redirect some of the savings toward paying down your debt, thereby increasing your credit score.

Several factors – including account history, late payment, available credit, credit usage, account balance and hard inquiries – affect your credit score. In order to see your credit score go up, you have to be current on your payments. Late payments on your light or water bill can negatively impact your credit score, although they do not increase your score if you pay them on time.

You can easily determine whether you are overutilizing your credit card simply by dividing your available credit card balance by the total credit card limit. For instance, if your credit card limit is $5,000 and you have a balance of $2,000 on your card, you are using 40% of your limit. That is too high. Some suggest that the optimal credit usage should be 30% or lower, but I believe that 30% is still a little too high.

When it comes to bad debts, you should always err on the side of conservatism, especially if you are already living paycheck to paycheck like 78% of American workers.[3] You should strive to keep your credit card utilization to around 10%. While that may sound like an unattainable goal for some, especially if your credit card debt is very high, applying some of the practical guides that I shared in this chapter can help you achieve that goal. The secrets to managing your spending are discipline and consistency.

Check your credit report at least once a year. Review your

report to confirm that there are no mistakes or identify theft. Knowing what's in your report is a great way to identify any unusual activities. Don't forget that financial discipline is a must. Live your life from the position of financial strength. Never tie debt around your neck – the weight of it will strangle you.

Adjusting your lifestyle now can be a powerful way to streamline your spending and potentially increase your savings and investment portfolios. If you resize now and manage your expenses well while you are financially viable, the extra cash should go towards your savings. If you have enough money in your savings account, you should consider investing some of that in both short-term and long-term investment portfolios.

Cut your coat according to your size now. Those who fail to cut their coats according to their sizes may be forced to go without one during personal financial crises.

Resize now or you may be forced to downsize soon. Now that you know how to resize and manage your spending, it is time to become debt free.

CHAPTER 6

DEBT FREE NOW

"...the borrower is slave to the lender." –The book of Proverbs.

Even the smartest of us have made some bad financial decisions. That was where my wife and I found ourselves around November and December of 2018. We learned the hard way that we never make any serious financial commitments based on money we thought we would get, but were not guaranteed to receive.

We were expecting to receive about $4,500 from two sources around December. Sadly, that never happened. What did happen, however, was that our credit card debt went up by more than $4,500. We made a few purchases during Black Friday and more around Christmas. Our thought was that we would incur about $1,500 in credit card debt and pay it off within two to three months, and then pay off the $4,500 debt once we receive the money that we were anticipating. No money came in and we were left with over $6,000 in credit card debt. By April of 2019, the total debt had ballooned to almost $10,000. Interest began to ratchet up. I'm talking about hundreds of dollars each month...

Debt is inevitable. If you've lived long enough, you can agree that you can't avoid debt completely. In fact, some debt can be a good thing. However, bad debts are bad news. They tend to lead into financial bondage, which can only worsen if you experience financial hardship due to recession. This chapter will be dedicated to the type of debts that have the tendency to cause trouble, as well as how you can address them before it is too late.

WHY YOU MUST BECOME DEBT-FREE NOW

Being debt-free before encountering recession will reduce the financial burden and decrease the risk of failing to meet your financial obligations. The stress of not being able to meet one's financial obligations can be immense. In fact, a research published in the Journal of Accountancy shows that too many Americans hate to owe; and they stress and worry about being in debts.[1]

Peace of mind during recession

Who says you can't survive and thrive during a recession? I believe you that can and will if you plan and prepare well. But if you can't meet your financial obligations because of shrinking finances, your creditors will be after you and you are likely to experience stress and lose your peace of mind. In fact, stress, if not controlled in time, can lead to other problems such as anger, depression, anxiety, drug and alcohol abuse, other health issues, and in some extreme cases, suicide. If you choose to become debt-free now, you will be far less likely to lose your peace of mind during recession. Remember that freedom from debt is just one of the weapons against recession and the crises that come with it. You must use this weapon in conjunction with others I discussed in this book.

Reduced financial obligations

For the sake of simplicity, assume that your current total financial obligations is $5,000 per month. Out of this number, recurring bad debts such as credit card debt and payday loans are $2,000 and the remaining $3,000 are mortgage, car loan and other essential expenses. If you go through a recession and sustain serious financial hardships, your monthly financial obligations will still be $5,000 (assuming your debts stay the same). It will be extremely difficult to continue to pay $5,000 each month without a stable income.

On the other hand, if you decide to pay off your credit card and other debts that require a monthly payment of $2,000, you will be left with only $3,000, which is more affordable than $5,000. In chapter 5, I covered in great detail why it is important to revisit your lifestyle now and look for areas where you may be overspending without even knowing it. Those who fail to become debt-free may be left with huge financial burdens that they will be unable to handle.

Extra cash flow to sustain you during recession

Let's continue with the example above. Say you paid off your bad debts and, now that you no longer make a monthly payment of $2,000, you decide to put all or some of that $2,000 into your savings account each month. By doing so, you will have a reasonable amount of money in your bank account to absorb any unexpected financial loss during recession. The less money you have to spend, the more you can save and potentially invest.

Creativity is the name of the game here. You must find creative ways to pay down your bad debts. The worst thing that can happen is to go into recession with massive debts. It will create undue stress that you may not be able to carry. Paying off your debt will free up your cash so that you can save more for rainy days.

Drastic bankruptcy risk reduction

If you can't meet your financial responsibilities, you are at risk of going bankrupt, which will force you to give up the essential things that support you and your family. During the Great Recession, thousands of families lost their homes in foreclosure. The majority of people had no choice but to file for bankruptcy. Losing the place where you call a home is anybody's worst nightmare. Everyone in the family feels the effect of it. But if you become debt-free now, you can avert the risk of going bankrupt if you were to lose your income.

TYPES OF DEBTS TO AVOID

Credit card debt

Credit card debt is one of the biggest bad debts that most American households carry. Low income earners and average middle-class workers are probably at the highest risk of defaulting on credit card debt at any time, particularly during recession. As of 2018, the average credit card debt in the United States was $9,333 and households with the lowest net worth (zero or negative) held an average of $10,308 in credit card debt.[2] In a simple term, your net worth is what you own (assets) minus what you owe (liabilities).

If you live from paycheck to paycheck and don't have any liquid assets, you may have a tough time taking care of your financial responsibilities during a crisis. Moreover, your debt is likely to increase if you fail to meet your financial obligations.

Defaulting on your credit card payments could result in higher interest and hefty penalties. If you use more than one credit card and you owe on each of them, you could be paying a substantial amount in interest. On top of that, if you miss a payment, you will be hammered with a penalty, and it can be high.

Car loans

Depending on your credit score, initial down payment and other factors, interest on car loans can be really high. My wife and I paid off our car loan on the car we currently drive in a record time. How did we do that? Anytime we received extra money outside of my normal pay check, such as a tax refund or unexpected paycheck, we put a portion of that money towards the principle. Approach your car loan the way you take on your credit card debt; find the strategy that works best for you and stick with it!

Personal loans

People take out personal loans for any number of reasons, such as a home remodel or major repairs, furniture, or a vacation. Just like any other debt, you will be required to pay interest on that loan, and the interest you get charged can vary from person to person.

Before you apply for the next loan, you might want to ask yourself whether you really need it. Can that project wait until you can afford it? Can you keep your vacation local this year and save up for a big one next year? If you can't afford it, why would you put yourself in a rough situation that can create serious financial strain and possibly trigger other personal crises?

Medical debt

One sad thing about medical debt is that it does not take too long to accrue. Just one emergency room visit can create an insane medical debt. All it takes is just one hospital admission to amass an unreal amount of medical bills. Trust me, we've been there, and it is not fun.

Granted, people go to the hospital for various reasons. Some instances are preventable while others might not be. Regardless, a single visit to a hospital can create a humongous financial burden for you. Your plan should be to invest in your health so that you don't get sick often or need to make frequent trips to the hospital.

If you happen to accrue medical bills, pay them down as soon as possible. You do not want to default on your medical bills. It can ruin your credit score. You can talk to the hospital and see if you can arrange some kind of assistance. Some hospitals, especially non-profit ones, have programs that can forgive most or all of your medical bills. The last thing that you want to be stressed about during a crisis is medical bills.

Other long-term payments

Two other debts to keep an eye on are mortgages and student loans. These types of debts are considered good debts because they can either appreciate in value (mortgage) or increase your earning potential in the future (student loans). Because these debts can run well into the thousands, they might place undue financial stress on you if you try to pay them off fast. However, you should bear in mind that these two debts can create big financial headaches for you during a recession.

The Great Recession caused more than 7.3 million consumers to lose their homes between 2007 and 2014.[3] If you have done everything else right – paid off debts, saved for rainy days, have passive income or thriving business – you should be able to handle the financial impact of a recession and would not need to worry about mortgage and student loan debts. Before you start pumping a lot of money on your student loans and mortgage, you should ensure that you have solid, diversified investments and solid savings. If you have extra money on hand, and all your other debt is paid off, by all means, pay down your student loans and mortgage.

If you apply all the guidelines above, you will be one step closer to averting the harm that recession causes. More importantly, if you work hard now to become debt-free, you will be in a better position to survive any personal financial crisis. Those who accumulate debts for whatever reason may risk losing everything they have worked for their entire life during a recession.

So, how did my wife and I overcome our credit card debt? After it shot up to almost $10,000, it dawned on us that something had to give. If you've been down this path, you know that it is a slippery slope that can lead you into a financial dungeon. Here are steps we took to get off our debt, and they are steps you can take too.

Cut back on expenses

Turn off lights when you don't need them. Increase the AC temperature a bit and make more use of fans during the summer. Put all that extra cash towards paying down the debt.

Statistics show that the average household in the United States wastes a substantial amount of water and energy. According to the Environmental Protection Agency, the average household wastes about 5,700 gallons per year just by letting their tap run while brushing their teeth and shaving.[4] Each person in the United States uses about 88 gallons of water every single day and pays about $70 extra per month.[5] Using these figures, you could possibly save $151.13 (or $604.55 for a family of four) dollars a year just by shutting off your tap while brushing your teeth.

While the majority of us like our lawns to look great, outdoor care is another area where people waste an insane amount of water. According to the EPA, if the average sized lawn in the United States is watered for 20 minutes every day for seven days, it's like running the shower constantly for 4 days or taking more than 800 showers. That's equivalent to the amount of water needed for the average family to take a year's worth of showers.[6]

These are just two examples of easy cost-cutting moves. Please note that I'm not advocating that you deprive yourself of what you enjoy. If you like to let the tap run while brushing, stay in the shower for a long time or water your lawn all year round and you can afford the bill, by all means, help yourself. I share these numbers to show you how you can save just by making simple adjustments that do not deprive you the opportunity to enjoy what you may consider essential for life. My wife and I had no choice but to cut back on how much water and energy we used in the house, and we channeled the extra savings toward our credit card debt.

Reallocate a portion of monthly savings towards debt

If you pay a high interest on your credit card balance and save regularly, consider reallocating a portion of your savings toward paying down credit card debt. You can increase your savings once you pay off your debts. My wife and I figured it would be unwise for us to save, say, $200 a month, and pay $150 in credit card interest each month. We decided to reallocate a portion of our monthly savings toward credit card debt. It was one of the best moves that we made.

Don't swipe your card if you don't have cash to pay for it

The hardest way to pay off any debt is to accumulate more while you are trying to pay it all down. While paying off your credit card debt, do everything necessary to limit adding extra debt. That's what my wife and I did. We put a control in place that we couldn't buy anything with a credit card if we didn't have the cash to pay for it. This meant deferring buying nonessential items; it called delayed gratification.

Reduce amount allocated to discretionary spending temporarily

If you are in debt and would like to become debt-free, you have two options: increase your income or adjust your spending. Obviously, increasing your income is always a better option, but when you can't increase your income, you have to resort to the second option.

In order to adjust your spending in such a way that your basic necessities of life aren't disrupted, you'll need to revisit your budget. My wife I and started paying off our credit card debts by making a spreadsheet and listing all the different credit cards we had and their balances. We began to pay them off starting from the credit card that had the high interest rate, which happened to the card with the highest balance. Ultimately, we paid off all the balances in other remaining cards in about a year. Part of it was readjusting how much we allotted to our monthly discretionary spending. We channeled the additional money towards paying down the credit card debt.

You have to remind yourself that the decision to cut back on discretionary spending is a better and wiser financial decision that pays off in the long run. Once you pay off your debt, you can always increase your spending, provided it is part of your budget and that you are not indebting yourself.

Having fun and enjoying life is one of the healthy ways to improve the overall quality of one's life. However, if you do it at the expense of your financial health, sooner or later your quality of life will diminish. A survey by the Journal of Accountancy showed that 73% of Americans have some type of debt. Interest payments on credit cards accounts for 30% of the debt. Vacations or luxury purchases make up 16% of the debt, and 56% said debt has a negative impact on their lives.[7] Save for your vacation and pay everything in full. That's what my family and I did to pay down our credit card debt. But we still had a fun vacation, and I enjoyed myself more because the extra cash went towards credit card debt.

The above approach are just a few ways to pay off debts. Don't be afraid to find other creative ways to tackle your credit card debts. Everybody's situation might be different and similarly, there are no hard-and-fast rules when it comes to paying off your debt. Perspectives about how to be debt-free might differ, but one thing is certain: carrying a huge amount of debt creates financial stress and hinders your ability to save and invest, without which, you can't attain financial freedom. In the end, it boils down to perspective and circumstance. Your perspective and your circumstance can play a part on how you to choose to address your debts. One thing you must not do is to do nothing. It is very costly. Choose to become debt free now or you might pay a non-negotiable price when a personal financial crisis strikes.

CHAPTER 7

SAVE NOW

"Do not save what is left after spending, but spend what is left after saving." –Warren Buffett.

"Never touch the lion by the tail, whether dead or alive, because you might not have the opportunity to tell the story." This saying perfectly described Meg until hardship began to hamper her agility and power. She appeared gentle, but if you provoked her, she would not give you a second to prove yourself. In her high school and college days, Meg was nicknamed "tiger" due to her aggression whenever someone provoked her. All her life, no one had ever brought any accusation against her for fomenting troubles. She was as quiet as she could be. But she visited the principal's office countless times for pulling hairs, scratching faces, and giving her victims pink eyes.

Meg loved to read books – especially science fiction – and she loved math. She followed the footsteps of her mother, a high school teacher who taught math and physics for 20 years before retiring in 2003. As the saying goes, the apple doesn't fall far from the tree. At a young age, Meg developed interest in math. After graduating high school, she decided to pursue her undergraduate degree in math, despite her Dad's opposition. In just three and half years Meg obtained her Bachelor's degree in math with a 3.9 GPA. She had multiple job offers from Fortune 500 companies, but her passion for teaching led her to reject those offers. Instead, she chose to teach math and physics at the high school where her mother taught for many years

Meg would say her choice to become a teacher was a divine orchestration. It was at a STEM fair that Meg met her husband, Kelly. Kelly was an actuary at one of the top insurance companies in the nation. They dated for about a year and decided to get married on Valentine's Day, 2004. Meg was the happiest person on the planet. It was a day she had longed for her entire life. After their wedding, she moved into her husband's San Francisco apartment. On February 24, 2006, Meg and Kelly welcomed their first child, Matt. Meg returned to her teaching job six months after Matt was born. Kelly, on the other hand, continued to work at the insurance company.

Although both couples shared a lot of things in common, they differed in their spending habits. Meg was frugal, but Kelly was extravagant. Kelly's favorite weekend getaway spots were casinos. Aside from drinking, gambling and sports betting were Kelly's favorite activities at the casinos. When not feasible to visit a casino, he engaged in an online gambling. Consequently, they had little savings and Meg was concerned that lack of sufficient savings could create serious financial strains in case of emergency. Often, the gambling behavior caused minor altercations between Kelly and Meg.

As the Great Recession loomed in late 2007, Meg started to worry that her husband's job could be affected, and that lack of lack sufficient savings could create financial hardship for them. Her worry eventually became a reality. Kelly lost his job on November 27, 2009, a day after Thanksgiving. As a high school teacher, Meg's salary was not sufficient to take care of their financial needs at home. As debt began to mount, so did pressure at home. Kelly held all his emotions inside, but you could tell he was struggling. Meg, on the other hand, was panicking. As days turned into months, Meg began to develop severe depression and anxiety. Kelly handled his stress differently. Instead of sharing his struggles with his wife and seeking ways to bounce back, he sought comfort from women as a means to cope with the financial stress.

It began as a casual Facebook chat with a friend. A casual chat turned into deep conversation and soon Kelly began cheating on his wife. When Meg found out, her combative personality that seemed to have melted into oblivion resurfaced. She went ballistic on her husband. When she confronted Kelly about his infidelity, he got upset and threatened to leave her. In anger, frustration and helplessness, Meg smacked Kelly across the face. Trouble ensued. It was a timely intervention by the next-door neighbor, who called the police, that saved the day.

Three days after the altercation, Kelly picked up a few of his personal items, left his apartment and never returned. Meg was left to pay all the bills and care for her three-year-old son, Matt. Meg was plagued by sleepless nights and severe panic attacks. The most embarrassing moment of her life was the day she attended a friend's wedding. As the thought of her failed marriage flooded her mind, the anxiety and panic attack were so bad that she passed out during the wedding. With the help of her mother and few friends, Meg continued to recover from the traumatic experiences she went through. Although she has not fully recovered to date, she has now learned to manage her anxiety. In 2017, Meg took a leap of faith and started dating again. His name is Luke.

WHY YOU SHOULD SAVE NOW

Setting aside a tangible sum of money is one of the most powerful weapons against recession. Having money that you can access in an emergency situation with less hassle can help dampen the impact of going through a crisis. So, if you currently do not have a savings account, take the first step and open one. If you have one but you do not save frequently, start setting aside a small amount each month.

There are types of savings accounts you should have: emergency savings (sometimes called a rainy day or emergency fund), short-term savings, long-term savings and health savings. What I share in this chapter will focus on savings that you can access with relative ease during emergencies. It does not matter how much you have in your account – if you can't withdraw from it when you urgently need it, or will incur severe penalties if you do so, then you may still experience financial hardships that come with a recession even though you saved some money. There are great benefits to setting aside some money that you can tap into during a recession.

Saving is your backbone against recession

Think of the money in your savings accounts as the foundation of a house. If you have a good and strong foundation, your house will not collapse, even during the worst storms. But if the foundation of your house is weak, it will collapse under pressure. When you do not have enough money to address your financial needs, especially during a recession, the foundation of your entire life might shatter. This is one of the reasons why anxiety and stress levels are high during recession. Adequate savings are the cornerstone for surviving and thriving during any personal financial crisis. Undoubtedly, having sufficient cash on hand is one of the most powerful weapons you have against recession.

Saving dampens the financial effect of recession

Have you ever seen a burning home or forest? I have. The fire rages uncontrollably, up until the fire department arrives. Then, the raging and stubborn fire gradually caves under the water's pressure. Depending on the severity of the fire and the amount of water, fire can burn for a moment or a while before it stops.

Think of recession as a raging fire and your cash on hand as the water. If you have enough money in your savings account, you can quench the fiery effect of the personal financial crisis. The more money you have the less effect of recession you might feel. If you don't have any savings at all, it may take you a very long time to dampen or slow the effect of recession. Just like fire that burns down a building, recession may char everything that you own and leave you with nothing. If you start saving now, you can dampen the effect of recession when it rages.

Saving reduces your chances of going under during recession

One of the major reasons many people get drowned in recession storms is because they did not have sufficient cash in their savings account. I'm sure you have heard that "money answers all things."[1] If you have millions of dollars in liquid assets when recession strikes, you may feel the effects of it slightly, but you will not drown yourself in debt.

Why do people worry, stress, and sometimes die during recession? One word: fear. Fear of what? Fear of not being able to meet financial needs. Fear of not paying their bills. Fear of losing their jobs, homes or cars. If you have saved a reasonable amount of money that can sustain you and your family for reasonable periods of time, you are more likely to have peace of mind than someone who does not have enough money to meet their needs. Those with foresight save, thus escaping the financial quagmire that recession brings. Those who fail to save crumble under the pressure of recession.

Saving gives you the negotiating power during recession

When you do not meet your financial obligations such as mortgage, car loans, and utility bills, you are likely to lose your basic amenities since you are obligated to pay for them. If, on the other hand, you have saved enough money, you can negotiate with your creditors or service providers. You can come up with payment arrangements that you can afford. Most creditor and service providers are likely to accept your offer and modify your monthly payment.

Take a mortgage for example. Many people lost their homes during the Great Recession. In just 2008, over 3.1 million foreclosure filings were issued and more than 860,000 families lost their homes to foreclosure the year before.[2] If you have sufficient cash in your bank account, you can request to pay interest only on your mortgage for a period of time until you are financially strong. That is much better than being foreclosed on. While making interest only payment on mortgage is certainly not desirable, it might be better to take that route during a recession, just for short periods of time. You could also have debt restructuring, which can include paying a lower interest rate or deferring payment.

HOW MUCH DO YOU NEED IN YOUR SAVINGS ACCOUNT?

The short answer is to save as much money as possible. However, how much you should have in your savings account can vary from person to person. It can also depend on whether you have short-term investments that you can liquidate easily to address urgent financial needs. Someone who has a huge financial obligation may need to save more than someone who has fewer financial responsibilities.

Ask yourself this: if recession were to strike and you lose

your job (and there are no other sources of income), how long would it take you to find another job? The U.S. Bureau of Statistics' March 2019 data shows that the average duration of unemployment was 22.9 weeks in 2019.[3] If you use this as a baseline, you should plan to have enough savings to cover your regular expenses for at least four to six months. That may sound like an impossible mission. You are probably correct. However, if you start saving now, you will get there quicker than you know.

The conventional recommendation is to save 20% of your monthly after-tax income.[4] Note that saving for retirement – such as a 401k – is included in that 20%. So, if you are already contributing to 401(k) or any other form of retirement savings you are already saving toward the 20% recommendation. For many people, 20% may be far-fetched, possibly unattainable. With healthcare cost skyrocketing, along with child care expenses, housing, food and transportation, it can be challenging for low-income earners, and even middle-class families, to allocate 20% of their income toward savings.

Saving for retirement is important, however, this chapter focuses on savings that you can access whenever you need it. You cannot tap into your retirement money without incurring a substantial fine, except in unique extenuating situations. If you are not saving for retirement, start now and take full advantage of your employer's 401(k) matching program, if your employer offers one. Do not leave any free money on the table.

In addition to saving for retirement, set aside a portion of your take home pay for savings. Start from somewhere and build from there. Start with what works for you.

HOW TO SAVE

If you currently don't have any money in your savings account, know that you are not alone. Nearly 70% of Americans have less than $1,000 in their savings account.[5] If you don't have any money in your savings account, one of the biggest hurdles you have to jump is taking that first step. If you save $50 per month, that amounts to $600 per year. If you save the same amount for 10 years, you have $6,000 in your savings account. $6,000 is better than not having money at all.

One of the major objectives of saving money is investing. If you see an investment opportunity that has the potential to yield a good return, consider diverting some of the money in savings toward the investment. Here are a few tips that can help you grow your savings account.

Start small

If you currently don't have any structure in place to save consistently, now is the time to have one. Just like paying your bills or buying things that you need, you should make savings a big part of your budget. Budget how much you want to save each month or each pay period. When you get paid, take that amount you budgeted for savings and put it in your savings account. Instead of personally transferring the amount you designate for saving to your savings account, make it an automatic transfer. Setting it and forgetting it ensures that you will never find an excuse to spend the money you should be saving.

For a long time, my family did not have a good structure in place to consistently save money. Basically, we saved after spending. Once we structured our savings, we saw a steady increase. At first, we were not saving a lot of money each month. But as soon as we paid down a few debts and streamlined our spending, we gradually increased how much we saved each month. Saving money requires discipline, discipline requires structure, and structure requires budgeting (as you read in chapter 5).

Automatic savings

Automatic savings is the most effective way to grow your savings. Automatic savings works just like your monthly payroll direct deposit. Instead of having your entire paycheck wired to your account, you can set up a separate account and direct a portion of your paycheck to the account you designated for saving. If you are a small business owner or a contractor, and you do not have the opportunity to utilize direct deposit, then you have to either physically deposit the amount you designated for saving or transfer it from your checking account to a savings account.

Have a separate account for your savings

It will be wise to open a separate savings account just for savings. You do not want to spend and then save what's left over. This might happen if you maintain one account for both savings and for other personal spending or paying bills. This was exactly what my wife and I did. And it works wonders!

Keep your savings account at a different bank

Another step you can take to ensure that you have enough money in your savings account is to open a savings account with a different bank. It might sound like an unnecessary step, but it is an important disciplinary measure to employ, especially if you have the history of dipping into your savings to cover nonessential expenses. If you have a checking and savings account with one bank, it will be easy to transfer money from one account to another. If you are putting money away for emergencies and investment opportunities only, you want to make it so hard to dip into your savings for frivolous reasons.

No ATM or Debit Card

When we opened our savings account, we intentionally declined both debit and ATM cards. Technology has made it so easy to transfer cash from bank to bank. If you urgently need cash, and don't want to drive to the bank to withdraw cash, you can transfer money from one account to another in just minutes. This is another way to add multiple layers of controls so you don't access your savings account for non-essential items. You must really need money from your savings account before making withdrawals. If you have an ATM or a debit card, you may not resist the temptation to swipe your card just because you ran out of money or need to make an "urgent" purchase. Not having a card will reduce impulsive spending from your saving account. Let your savings serve the specific purpose you set it up to serve.

Not long ago, my car broke down and I had to repair it. It cost me about $800 to fix the problem. How did I take care of the unexpected expense? I paid the repair cost with my credit card, and electronically transferred $800 to my checking account from my savings account, which I maintain at a different bank. As soon as the money reflected on the checking account, I paid off the credit card. This approach has helped us a lot to put more money into our savings account. Following this approach will help you build a disciplined saving habit. If you have to take some drastic steps such as declining an ATM or debit card for your savings account in order to avoid making frequent withdrawals, thereby ensuring that your savings account steadily increases, that is a win-win in my book.

THE 40/60 RULE

The 40/60 rule simply means that if you happen to receive

any unexpected money, save 40% of it and spend or invest the remaining 60%. This is a great way to grow your savings. Thanks to the 40/60 rule, we have seen an increase in our savings

People save money for various reasons – everything from preparing for emergencies or major life events to paying down debt. The one major reason why you should have money that you can withdraw without any hassle is to take care of any unexpected financial obligations. Secondly, you should save in order to invest. It is almost impossible to invest if you don't save. Obviously, investment is more than just 401k, stocks and bonds. You can invest in your own business. You can partner with someone and start a business. Also, you can invest in real estate, and the list goes on. Some lucrative investment opportunities may come up when you least expected them. If you have cash on hand, you can take advantage of such opportunities. Cash-strapped people struggle, but the deep-pocketed thrive during recession. What makes the difference? Preparation. Prepare now by saving so that you can not only survive during a personal financial crisis, but thrive.

CHAPTER 8

INVEST IN YOUR HEALTH NOW

"The greatest and the most rewarding investment you can make is in your health, because everything you do in this life is done in or through your body." –Nonso Okpala.

Mira was the most charming lady you will ever meet. Her work ethic was second to none. She attributed her hard work and courage to her grandfather, who owned a small farm in upstate New York before he passed away many years ago. Mira learned from Papa that hard work and strong work ethic both pay off. That piece of advice she received when she was 11 years old shaped her view about life and career.

Shortly after her parents divorced, Mira moved to Lancaster, Pennsylvania and lived with her Mom. She went to college and graduated summa cum laude. Upon graduation, Mira attended law school, passed her bar exam, and landed a job at a regional law firm in Pennsylvania. She was one of the few female lawyers at the firm at the time and was the youngest lawyer at the firm. Her age did not deter her from rubbing shoulders with her peers and superiors.

Truly, Mira was an embodiment of intelligence. That, coupled with her hard work, made her almost invincible. She won many cases and amassed both regional and national awards. She speedily and steadily climbed the corporate ladder. Moreover, Mia broke her law firm's 50-year record when she became the first person to make partner in just four and half years. The icing on the cake for Mira was that she reached that momentous accomplishment at the age of 28. Indeed, Mira's life was the epitome of perfection…almost.

Despite her beauty, well-built physique, and charming personality, Mira had neither a boyfriend nor a husband. Her work was her life, family and friends. Outside of a few colleagues, Mira did not have any true friends in her life. It wasn't that she didn't want friends – she just didn't have the time. After a few colleagues at work encouraged her to get a pet, she reluctantly bought a cat named Lucky. That relationship lasted for just three weeks. She took Lucky to the local animal shelter because she did not have time to take care of a pet.

Mira worked seven days a week. Even on major holidays, she was at the office. After winning a case that attracted major media attention, Mira bragged about getting just four hours of sleep each night. Coffee and sugar were her go-tos. Except for going to lunch or dinner with colleagues and clients, Mira lived off fast food and restaurants virtually her entire career. Taking care of her health was a low priority for her. She worked so hard that she did not make time for things that promote health and happiness.

Mira had a rude awakening on July 27, 2010, after she was promoted to managing partner at the law firm. She woke up with severe pain in her chest and neck. It was so bad that she had to visit the ER. Her ER visit showed that she had coronary artery blockages and a beyond abnormal cholesterol level. Three weeks after visiting the ER, Mira was in the operating room for an open-heart surgery. As you might expect, recovery was slow, but she was not ready to give up just yet. She continued to work hard, but her health issues kept slowing her down.

At the age of 50, Mira was forced to retire due to cognitive decline. She was diagnosed with early-onset dementia at the age of 48. In just five years, Mira spent her entire life's savings to fight her dementia. Sadly, all the wealth that she accumulated could not help her. The more she fought her dementia, the worst it progressed. At the age of 53, Mira could not care for herself anymore. She could barely remember her name. Today, Mira lives in a nursing home. She has no one else to take care of her and no relatives to visit her.

GET YOUR HEALTH IN ORDER NOW

Recessions can cause personal financial crises, and those crises can adversely affect your health. If you already have an underlying health condition, it may get worse if you experience financial hardship. Think of strengthening your health now as wearing a bulletproof vest. Experiencing a sudden financial crisis is like getting shot in the chest. With a bulletproof vest on you, you might feel the impact slightly, but the bullet won't penetrate your chest.

Prepare for a personal or global recession by investing in your health. You have a higher chance of surviving the economic impact of recession if you have solid health. In fact, you may not feel any impact on your health if you take action now and give your health a boost.

In my opinion, investing in your health now is the most important way to prepare for a crisis. Why? The last thing you want to encounter while going through any personal financial hardship is a health crisis too. Combining health problems with financial hardship could increase your risk of dying early. Stress, anxiety and depression can compromise your immune system and put you at risk for heart disease, high blood pressure and any other number of physical and mental ailments. Adding health challenges to financial pressure is a double whammy, one you would want to avoid at all costs. It all begins with prioritizing your health and investing in it now.

WHY YOU SHOULD INVEST IN YOUR HEALTH NOW

If health is wealth, then it makes sense to invest in it now. Not tomorrow, and certainly not during a recession. If you've invested in your health, it will pay off during a crisis. All you need to do is keep applying what works and what promotes good health. If you don't have any plan in place, you can still start from somewhere, but it's much harder to start from scratch when you have a major crisis at hand. Also, if you've invested in your health well enough, you will have more strength and sanity to absorb the shock created by any crisis.

YOUR VITAL FORCE IS KEY

Think of your vital force as your health savings account, and your health as your bank account. If you deposit money in your account, you can make withdrawals anytime you need it. The more money you put in, the more withdrawals you can make. If you stop depositing money in your bank account, you can still withdraw until the money runs out. If you've deposited a lot of money in your bank account, it might take a long time to deplete the account.

Similarly, when you prioritize and invest heavily in your health, you are making a deposit into your health bank account. Anytime you need to make a withdrawal, you'll be assured that there is something in the account. Recessions can create severe financial struggles, stress and anxiety, in addition to other issues. If you have strategized well and applied other guides that I share throughout this book, your recession might not last very long. Even if it does, you will survive and not drown in the deep ocean of financial struggles and you won't completely deplete your health savings account. Don't be like Mira: she depleted her health savings account so badly that her real retirement savings could not save her from dementia.

HOW TO INVEST IN YOUR HEALTH

There are several things that can affect your health, such as your environment, diet, stress level and sleep. To live healthy, be healthy, and stay healthy, you have to understand that there is no one size fits all. You must understand that you are unique. What nourishes you may not nourish the other person. Moreover, several factors such as your age, cultural background, race, and state of mind can affect your health. Nonetheless, there is a general consensus that, regardless of the factors I mentioned above, there are key principles you should consider if you want to be healthy.

Please note that the information below is not health advice. It is always advisable to consult your health professional before you make any serious changes to your diet or health, especially if you have any underlying health conditions. These are general health tips that are known to improve quality of life.

Nutrition

You are what you eat, period! Anything that goes into your mouth can either nourish you or diminish your health. If it is true that you are what you eat, then you must carefully choose what you put inside your body.

1. Increase your intake of plant-based foods; they are rich in Omega 3 and 6 fatty acids. If you eat animal products, organic, pastured animal products are the best.

2. Variety, variety, variety. Diversification is important. Eating a variety of vegetables and fruits is a great way to get essential vitamins, minerals, antioxidants, and fiber.
3. Limit your sugar intake. Excessive sugar consumption can be damaging to your health.
4. Consider juicing. Drinking freshly-juiced vegetables is one of the fastest ways to get all the essential nutrients and vitamins into your body.
5. Feed your gut. The majority of your immune systems live there and an unhealthy gut can lead to digestive issues, autoimmune diseases, sleeping problems and food allergies.[1] To repair or improve your gut health, try prebiotic (garlic, onion, leek, asparagus) and probiotic (fermented) foods. Also, minimize stress. If you are constantly stressed, your immune system may become weak at some point and can expose you to numerous health issues.
6. Minimize your intake of processed foods. Many processed foods contain additives and preservatives that are harmful to the body.
7. Eat most of your food whole. Whole foods are foods that have been minimally processed, if they have been processed at all. By eating whole foods, you are providing your body with all the essential nutrients and enzymes it needs. Whole foods include vegetables, fruits, unprocessed meats, nuts, legumes, seeds, and grains.
8. Don't forget to read food labels. Your health depends on it. You need to know what's in the food that you eat.

Exercise

A lack of physical activity can lead to severe health problems such as cardiovascular diseases and brain-related diseases like dementia, as well as other host of diseases. Regular exercise can lower both stress and blood pressure levels. If you have not been exercising, start today.

Generally, when beginning an exercise regime, you should start small and gradually increase how long you exercise. You can start as low as five to 10 minutes per day and increase to 30 minutes four to five times a week. It doesn't have to be vigorous; a brisk walk counts. Mowing your lawn and gardening are two other great ways to exercise. Anything that gets your heart rate up and your body moving is better than nothing!

Also, avoid sitting down for too long. Did you know that sitting for too long can block oxygen-rich blood from circulating well in your body, particularly your brain?[2] Sitting for too long does more harm than good to your body. This can lead to chronic back pain, muscle atrophy, and heart diseases. For every hour of sitting, move for about 10 minutes. Research has shown that even regular exercise may not compensate for the harmful effect of excessive sitting.[3]

Sleep

Have you ever wondered why you are encouraged to get enough sleep when you are sick? Sleep gives your body the opportunity to heal itself. During sleep, your body channels the energy towards repairing itself, removing toxins built up in the body. A lack of adequate sleep has been linked to cognitive decline, weight gain, aging fast, depression, and other chronic diseases.[4]

It may be easier said than done, but try to get seven hours of sleep a night. Create an environment that makes it easy to fall asleep. This could include limiting your screen time a few hours before bedtime, removing electronic devices from your bedroom, keeping your bedroom neat and organized, turning off lights in your bedroom before going to bed, and using your bedroom solely for sleeping and personal time with your spouse.

Air

Fresh quality air improves the lungs. Try to receive fresh air regularly; get outside and inhale the fresh air, quit smoking, and keep plants in your house. Be sure to open your windows for at least 10 minutes each day. Poor air quality can have an adverse effect on your health. If necessary, keep an air purifier at home, especially where you spend most of your time and where kids sleep. Be sure to clean your home regularly, especially the items that can collect and emit dust and toxins, such as electronics, carpet and kitchen appliances.

Water

Growing up, my mother always told me, "Drink water because water is life." Now that I am older, I understand and appreciate that piece of advice more than I did when I was young. Let water be your companion!

Inadequate water intake has been linked to brain damage, constipation, premature aging and blood pressure issues.[5] Typically, when your body lacks sufficient water, it will pull water from less critical parts of the body – such as bones – and supplies it to critical parts such as heart and brain. Obviously, if your bones lack the optimal amount of water needed to function well, the symptoms will manifest in the form of pain and aches. Drink a lot of water for good mood, proper digestion, toxin removal from the body, and prevention of arthritis.[6]

The amount of water you should drink in a day depends on several factors such as your age, state of your health, level of physical activity, among others. To determine how much water to drink in a day, divide your body weight by 2, and that's the total ounce of water you should drink. Someone who weighs 200 lbs. (90 kg) will need about 100 ounces of water per day.

Don't drink a large amount at once, sip it throughout the day. Your body can only use a certain amount at once, and discard the rest.

Sunlight

Despite the consistent rising and setting of the sun, 80% of Americans are deficient in vitamin D.[7] The health implications of vitamin D deficiency could be severe, anything from heart disease, multiple sclerosis, hypertension, diabetes, depression, bone issues, and asthma.

There are few factors that can affect your vitamin D level. To get vitamin D from the sun, you have to expose your body directly to the sun's UV. Unfortunately, some parts of the world do not have enough sunshine in any given year. This can pose some health issues for you. Those who live farther away from the equator (the center of the earth) may not get adequate sun throughout the year. Vitamin D supplementation can be of great benefit if you are not getting adequate sunlight or your vitamin D level is low.

Other than location, your age can affect how much UV your body can absorb from the sun. The older you get, the less vitamin D your body can absorb from sunlight. Your health conditions can play a part in your body's ability to absorb vitamin D from the sun. People with underlying health conditions may have a hard time synthesizing vitamin D from the sun. Additionally, your skin color is another factor. Those with darker skin color may take longer time to absorb vitamin D from the sun than those with fair skin color. People with dark skin have more melanin and this compound is known to slow down the production of vitamin D in the body. On the other hand, if you have a fair skin color you will get sunburn faster than someone with dark skin.[8]

When it's not possible to get enough sunlight, you should consider a vitamin D supplement, especially during the winter season. Some notable health experts recommend that you do not take vitamin D supplements alone. Instead, they recommend that you take it with vitamin K2. Vitamin D helps your bone absorb calcium, which is essential for healthy bones. Vitamin K2 serves as the vehicle that takes calcium to your skeletons, but prevents calcium from building up in other parts of the body where you do not need it, especially your arteries.[9]

Aside from sun and supplements, you can get a small amount of vitamin D naturally from some fish, mushrooms, and egg yolks.[10] Alternatively, you can consume certain foods that are fortified with vitamin D. You just have to be careful that the food is actually healthy and isn't loaded with additives and preservatives that are harmful to the body. Finally, you should check your vitamin D level (25-Hydroxy D) at least once a year.

Spirituality

Having some type of spiritual connection has been shown to have a positive impact on our health. For some, connecting with a higher power through prayers, songs, scripture or other means help them deal with life uncertainties. Some people who trust in divine power cope with life's challenges such as recession much better.

We all know that exhaustion and burnout are major problems in our fast-paced world today. Setting aside time to connect with God, family, friends, and nature is important to living a healthy and happy life.

Relationship

Building a strong and vibrant relationship with your spouse, family and friends can increase the quality of your life. Invest in it, and your body will thank you for doing so. When you are in a thriving relationship, you experience happiness and peace. Your stress level goes down. People in toxic relationships report heightened levels of fear, anxiety, and depression.

If you need to repair broken relationships, build new relationships or strengthen waning ones, now is the best time to do it. It really does not matter how healthy you eat; if you experience constant fear and anxiety due to relationship problems, your health will suffer.

Career

Your career will always have a way of impacting your health. If you have a thriving career and are satisfied with what you do, it will reflect positively on your health. People who are not engaged or happy with their job tend to experience more stress and anxiety. Gallup's 2017 World Poll found that 70% of American workers are not engaged at work.[11] The more disengaged you are at your workplace, the more likely you are to experience stress and dissatisfaction with your job.

You want a career that fulfills you; the more fulfilled you are the happier you will become with what you do. If you are not satisfied with your job, you should find the root cause, first. Wrong career? Personal issues? Bad boss? Clearly define the problems in order to find a lasting solution. Take Japan; a whopping 94% of workers are not engaged at work, and there are high stress, burnout, and suicide rates.[12] No doubt, your career impacts your health. If y you wake up each day dreading about going to work, chances are that your job is not fulfilling you. Invest in a career that fulfills you.

I will end this chapter by reminding you that you must prioritize your health and invest in it now. If you do so now, you will reap the benefits both now and in the future, especially during a personal financial crisis. Following the steps outlined above will put a good model in place for a healthy and happy life. That is the recipe for a long and healthy life.

CHAPTER 9

SPIRITUALITY NOW

Faith and prayer are the vitamins of the soul; man cannot live in health without them." –Mahalia Jackson.

Shortly after my wife and I got married, we decided to have kids right away. After a few months of trying, nothing happened. We tried for a few extra months but she did not conceive. At that point we knew that it was time to see a fertility specialist. We made multiple hospital visits and my wife was prescribed medications. Still, no success.

Finally, the doctor referred us to see a radiologist to ensure that my wife didn't have any blockage in the fallopian tube. That was where our nightmare began. The radiologist didn't provide much information but informed us that there was no flush out, meaning that my wife's fallopian tubes were blocked. He referred us back to the primary doctor for the full result. Tears rolled down my wife's face as we drove home; and we said no words to each other for more than 10 minutes. Surely, it was a sober and dark moment for us. It was difficult for me to find the right words to speak to my wife

More bad news awaited us during that appointment when

the doctor confirmed that my wife's fallopian tubes were blocked and that it won't be possible for her to get pregnant. Our hearts dropped. There was silence in the room for a few seconds and then…

We've talked about spirituality briefly in previous chapter, but let's dig a little bit deeper into why you must add it to your recession preparation and readiness toolkit.

WHY SPIRITUALITY NOW?

Recession can make the strongest and the bravest among us feel weak and cowardly. When recession strikes suddenly, it can feel like falling from a 1,500-foot-high mountain all the way down to the valley below. If you don't have the right implements, your fall can be devastating. That's where spirituality comes in. You need that cushion to make the impact of the fall less painful.

Being a spiritual person does not make you immune from a recession or from suffering the financial impact of a recession. Unfortunately, recession is a part of being human and living in an imperfect world. My wife and I did not bargain for the infertility struggle and the financial strain that came with them. Whatever yours might be, or may be in the future, one thing that will help you survive during your recession is having that spiritual anchor.

Personally, I believe that some of the issues associated with recession can be mitigated by placing your faith and trust in God. For my wife and I, our faith in God helped us tremendously during those dark days. If you've been down that path, you understand the pain that infertility can bring. Each spouse might deal with their infertility differently, but in our case, it was harder on my wife than on me. If you haven't experienced infertility, I hope it never comes your way, but if it does, hopefully our story will encourage you not to give up or take it out on your spouse.

Whatever your recession is, know that seeking spiritual support will help you deal with the impact in a more reasonable way. I have mentioned it countless times, but now is the time to prepare. Don't wait until recession strikes to empower yourself spiritually. If you don't have a solid spiritual foundation, you may still survive your recession by using the other tools in this book. But having a strong connection with a higher power will help you get through your recession much better.

Someone might ask, "If you believe in God, why didn't He unblock your wife's fallopian tubes or make the issue go away?" I hate to disappoint you, but I don't have an answer for you. But I will tell what I do believe. I believe that God is aware of my problems. If He allows me to go through hardship, it will turn out for my good in the end.

As humans, we hate pain. We get angry when we experience it and sometimes, we look for someone to blame for our pain and suffering. Unfortunately, pain and suffering are a part of life. You hope, wish, and pray that you do not suffer much in your lifetime, but they do come and will come. Going through a divorce can be painful. Losing a child or a loved one is painful. Losing a job is painful. However, you will recover if you persevere when you experience these types of recessions. Having strong faith can help make the journey more bearable. Add spirituality to your toolbox today, not tomorrow. My wife and I had it before we got struck by the recession of infertility and it got us through.

Our Infertility Journey Continues

After breaking the bad news to my wife and I, the doctor offered two solutions: adoption or IVF. IVF was very expensive at the time – around $15,000 – and we could not afford it because our insurance didn't cover it. As I sat and listened to the doctor, I mentally rejected those two options. I never doubted that my wife would become pregnant.

It was a somber moment for us, especially for my wife. I felt helpless. I'm a problem-solving type of guy, but this problem was insurmountable for me. I could not solve the problem. So, we turned to God for help. Many nights my wife would wake up and cry. I watched her mood change anytime she saw a pregnant woman; it wasn't jealousy, just longing. It was truly a tough personal recession for us. Multiple hospital visits aren't cheap, and the infertility recession also created financial hardships for us.

I remember the day we left the radiologist office. My wife was crying as we were driving home. I remember telling her that the doctor had reported what they saw, but God has the final say in this matter, and that nothing was impossible with God. We spent a lot of time in prayer. We prayed, we fasted, and we stood on God's promises.

Our faith in God kept us together. We were not mad at or frustrated with one another. We continued to work with the fertility specialist, but we did not opt for IVF or adoption. A few months later, my wife became pregnant with twins. We have been blessed with three beautiful kids.

How did it happen? How did the blocked fallopian tubes open? In a word, GOD. We believe that He answered our prayers.

I don't know how, when, and why He answers some prayers and not others. There have been times I have experienced some other personal recessions that I prayed to God about, but God did not answer my prayers when and how I wanted them answered. While our story ended with my wife getting pregnant and having kids. For other couples, their similar prayers may not be answered the same way. Their answered prayer might be adoption.

If you want to survive and potentially thrive during your recession, you must fortify yourself spiritually now. There are few benefits to being close to God and having a strong spiritual footing during crises.

Spirituality helps make your recession journey bearable

I remember hearing about a story of an individual who accused God of abandoning him whenever he was in a difficult situation. He observed that whenever things were going well, he would turn back and see two sets of footprints behind him, his and God's. But when difficult challenges surfaced, he would see only one set of footprints. He was angry that God abandoned him in a time of crisis. God responded to this by showing the young man that those footprints were God's; God had stepped in and carried the man through difficult times. When the situation improved, the young man began to walk again, and he saw two sets of footprints again.[1]

I recognize that spirituality may mean different things to different people, but it has been proven that those who have some type of spiritual connection with God handle difficult situations better.

Surely, trust in divine power does not make you immune from life's difficulties. However, it does help you have the right perspective about your situation. It helps you recognize that someone higher than yourself knows about your difficulties. And that gives you hope that regardless of the outcome of your predicament, you are not alone.

I mentioned in Chapter 1 how the great recession of 2007 - 2009 impacted so many lives negatively. People lost their jobs, homes, health, and lives. Some chose to soothe their pain through alcohol and drugs. Others succumbed to the pressure of their adversity and gave up hope, resulting in serious health problems. Still others saw their situations as bleak or hopeless and decided to take their own lives. One thing is common in these cases: a lack of hope.

Losing hope is like finding yourself in a dark hole with no light and no rope or ladder for you to use to climb out. Conversely, when you find yourself in a dark hole and you have faith that somehow help will come, that is hope. You might suffer for a while and fear for your life every now and then, but you never lose the drive to fight for your life, survive your hardships, and come out of your recession. Anchoring your faith in God will help you bear the fear, stress, and pain of recession. It helps you believe that there is a light at the end of the tunnel.

Spirituality helps you stay focused

People deal with financial stress differently. Some suffer in silence while some seek help from other people; others express their struggle in negative ways such as violent behaviors and alcohol or drug abuse. Still others turn to God for help.

One thing is certain: if you attempt to address a difficult situation in your life in a negative way, it will result in more problems for you. However, staying spiritually strong will keep you focus on the issue at hand. When my wife and I went through our infertility crisis, we focused on the issue, prayed about it and looked for professional help. We were able to put the problem into perspective. It was nobody's fault. There was no blame game. There was no finger pointing. We knew that if we came together, we had no time to fight against one another. We knew that if we emboldened ourselves spiritually, we would have the strength to strike back our enemy rather than striking at each other.

To win your recession battle, you must remain focused. You must keep your eyes on your enemy – recession – and on your faith for spiritual strength. Recognize that your recession is a battle that you must fight firmly and aggressively, and be well-equipped to wage a relentless and ruthless battle to survive it. It all starts by empowering yourself spiritually.

I remember one strange dream I had. I saw myself on a very dark, small path. I could barely see anything and, as you might guess, I was terrified. I faintly saw someone walking along that dark path. The more I focused on the individual walking, the more frightened I became. Suddenly, I saw a light shine on the opposite side of the dark path. It caught my attention, and I began to look toward that light. As I gazed at the light, I became less fearful. There were a few times in that dream that I attempted to look away, toward the dark path, but I would hear a voice in my head nudging me to focus on the light.

Recession is like that dark path. If you focus all your attention and energy on the trouble it brings, you will become fearful. The longer you dwell on it the more fearful you will become. That fear will drive you to make decisions you might later regret or that might cause harm to you and to the people around you. On the positive side, if you focus your eyes on the light – which I believe represents divine strength – you might still struggle, but you will survive your recession.

Spirituality helps you maintain a positive outlook

Spirituality can help you embrace your challenges with a positive mindset. Shifting your mindset will help you recognize that your difficult times are not permanent. I heard about this story many years ago. I have told it to myself whenever I go through tough times and I have encouraged others with it. I hope it reminds you that having a positive outlook on life in light of your situation is a sure way to survive your recession.

A man and his son set out on a journey. The son drives the car and his dad sits in the passenger seat. The weather is beautiful – the sun is shining and the sky is blue. Several miles into their journey, the sun ceases to shine, and the sky turns dark. A few minutes later, it begins to rain so hard they could barely see the car in front of them. The son panics and becomes afraid. He turns to his dad, expecting to see the same reaction, but is surprised: his dad looks completely calm and peaceful.

Out of trepidation, the son asks for his dad's permission to stop the car and park on the side of the road. The dad responds by telling his son to keep driving. As they drive through the storm, several cars stop and are overtaken by the rising water.

Seeing this, the son begs his dad to let him stop multiple times, but his dad assures his son that soon they will pass through the storm and there would be sunshine on the other side of the town.

Sure enough, it isn't long before the two make it through the storm. The sun shines again and the sky is clear. In a low voice, the dad asks the son to stop if he wants to. The son is amazed that his dad would ask him to stop only after the storm was over. In response, the dad reminds his son that all the people who stopped along the road were still in the storm, but the two of them were on the other side, in the sunshine.[2]

Know that your storm won't last forever if you don't give up. Remember that the sun will shine again. Build up your faith and empower yourself spiritually so you can weather any storm that recession sends your way. Don't procrastinate. Don't push it off. Don't wait until tomorrow. It might be too late.

CHAPTER 10

STRONG SUPPORT NETWORK NOW

"You can't live entirely alone. You have to have some kind of a support system" –Wendell Berry.

Meet Sara and Steve, siblings who were born and raised in Chicago, Illinois. Sara was born in 1988 and Steve was born two years later in May 1990.

Sara and Steve fit the description of "good kids" to a tee. They were raised in church. Their parents set good moral standards from a young age; some people might describe them as "strict." Sara and Steve were not allowed to watch TV for more than an hour a day, and they were never allowed to play video games. While Steve and Sara were not very pleased with their parents' disciplined way of parenting, they respected and honored their parents. Steve loved and admired his Dad, and always said he wanted to be just like his father when he grew up. In the same way, Sara was mommy's girl, a replica of her Mom - in both character and in physique.

Steve's Dad was well respected at his job. He was an accountant at a local CPA firm. His advice to his kids was always to honor and treat everyone with respect and "be the first to show up to work and be the last to leave." Sara's Dad loved his wife so much that he would never argue with her, even when serious issues came up, but would wait until Steve and Sara went to bed to have a reasonable discussion. Steve and Sara observed how Dad treated them and how he honored and respected their Mom. You can understand why both Steve and Sara were heartbroken when their Dad's health began to fail him, and how deeply wounded and scared they became when tragedy struck.

Steve was a freshman in college and Sara was a sophomore when they received the traumatizing call from their Mom. "Your Dad just passed away." Steve's Dad died of a heart attack on September 14, 2009. The Great Recession had a severe impact on the firm where he worked, and he was one of the last people the firm laid off. Losing his job was hard for him to handle, and his failing health worsened the situation for him. He died exactly one week and two days after losing his job.

After his father's death, Steve completely lost it. His superhero was gone. His role model was no more. Sara struggled too. The death of their Dad created a huge vacuum in their lives, and Steve and Sara were unable to cope. Steve stopped attending classes and dropped out of school halfway through his second semester of his freshman year. His mental health suffered and he began to use and abuse drugs to cope. Because he could not sustain himself and his new habit, Steve joined a local gang that robbed people and broke into homes.

Sara, on the other hand, stayed in school but struggled to focus. However, the help and support that she received from friends and her university's counselling office helped her cope with the loss of her Dad. She stayed connected with her Mom (while Steve would go for months without calling or visiting home) and continued to fight through her adversity. Sara graduated with a decent GPA and landed a job as a mental health counselor at a local hospital.

Sadly, Steve's life continued to tumble. Despite numerous attempts by his Mom and Sara to help, he refused. On January 5, 2013, Steve was arrested for armed robbery and illegal drug possession. A few months later he was convicted and sentenced to fifteen years in prison.

Do you have a strong community you can run to for support whenever you experience a recession? You want a tested and trusted group of people with whom you can share your personal struggles and be assured that they won't gossip about your struggles or pass judgement on you.

Tragedies and hardships have ways of making fools of us. Even the most enlightened and disciplined can succumb to the pressure of financial hardships and other struggles that result from recession. Some people tend to make impulsive and irrational decisions when they go through struggles in life. Stress, fear, and anxiety can impact your ability to think clearly and make informed decisions. As you can see in the story of Steve, he felt like the best way of dealing with his personal recession was to engage in gang activities, and ultimately armed robbery. Steve's family, especially his Mom and sister suffered emotionally from that singular action, and will probably suffer for a very long time. That's why you need a group of die-hard folks to lean on and help steer you in the right path while maintaining your sanity until you can get on your feet again.

If you're looking for this support when you're already in a crisis, chances are that you may fall into the wrong hands or share your struggles with people who may take advantage of you because you're desperate and possibly defenseless. Personally, I have five strong communities or support networks, and I'm confident that I can come to them in times of need. Because they have been tested and have proven trustworthy, I can share my struggles with them. I know I can lean on them for support.

WHY YOU NEED A SUPPORT NETWORK NOW

The Okinawa people in Japan have one of the highest life expectancies and "disability free-life" rates in the world.[1] Their longevity is attributed, in part, to their strong social support networks. The Okinawans have a deep-rooted culture of having strong social networks that "lend financial and emotional support in times of needs and give all of their members the stress-shedding security of knowing that there is always someone there for them."[2]

Some people can have a community of people who will stand by them sometimes, but such a community may not always promote positive messages or behaviors. For example, if you have good buddies with whom you drink alcohol on a regular basis, it may not work in your favor to seek their support in a time of crisis. As I noted in chapter one, drinking oneself into a stupor, especially in time of crisis, is not a good idea. It exposes you to a host of other problems – disease, domestic violence, or exposing yourself or others to serious injuries or death from accidents. This statement from the book of Proverbs sums up my point here: "Confidence in an unfaithful man in time of trouble is like a broken tooth, and a foot out of joint."[3] You need a community that can pull you up, not push you down. You need a support system that can help you get out of your problems and not create extra problems for you.

A strong community can be a life-saver. You do not want to blow it off. Invest in it now, and it will pay off big-time when you are caught in a financial crossfire. Your support system can be the deciding factor in whether you will survive or succumb to recession when it comes your way. People who don't have good support in their lives tend to experience more depression than those who have support; if you are already dealing with stress, anxiety or depression, it may get worse when you are in a crisis. Therefore, invest in a strong community now who would help you deal with your recession when it comes.

WHAT TYPE OF SUPPORT NETWORKS DO YOU NEED?

The popular quote, "no man is an island"[4] sums up why you need a support network. We are all guaranteed to experience crises at some point in our lives. For that reason, you need people to lean on. You may not survive on your own when you are experiencing financial struggles, and even if you do survive on your own, your recovery might be slower, more painful, and more stressful than it would be if you had a strong community around you. There is an African adage that says, "When an animal needs to scratch its back, it goes to a tree, but when humans need to scratch their backs, they go to fellow humans." I hope you get the point. You don't have to suffer alone. You don't have to die in silence. You must have a circle of trusted community that you can open up to about your struggles, and trust that you won't be disappointed or taken advantage of.

When searching for a support group, ask yourself one vital question: "If I go through a personal recession (job loss, financial hardship, unexpected serious health diagnosis, loss of a loved one, divorce, etc.), would my network be there for me, cry with me, guide me, believe for me, encourage, and provide or recommend resources that will help me get through recession until I'm back on my feet?"

If you currently have a community, would your answer to the above question be a resounding "yes"? If so, you are on your way to surviving and thriving during tough economic times, provided you apply other guides that I shared in this book. If your answer is "no" or "maybe" you need to invest in a strong support network or community now. You need it now, because it could be the glue that keeps your life from falling apart during any crisis.

As you may know, you are most vulnerable at the lowest point in your life. For many people, that low point comes in the form of a recession. No one likes to feel vulnerable; we all struggle with sharing our problems because they make us feel exposed. This is another reason why you must invest in a community now: a community that you can trust; a community that you believe in; a community that you feel safe to share your struggles with and feel confident that you won't be taken advantage of; and a community that won't let you down when you need it the most.

Another important point to note is that your support network will change as you progress through life. Some of your networks will change. Some will be there for a very long time, if not your entire life. My support networks range from an individual to groups of people. Each of these communities are very important to me, all for different reasons. You may not need the support of your entire community for every crisis that you encounter, and knowing the type of crisis you are facing will help you decide who you need to talk to. Do you need material support such as money or a place to stay temporarily? Do you need emotional or spiritual support? Do you just need a listening ear, encouragement, or advice?

Even with the right support network, sharing your crisis with the wrong audience may not lead you to the help and support that you desperately need. Ultimately, you are the right person to decide who you should involve. The following are the list of support networks that I have leaned on in times of crises. Add these to your own list and do not hesitate to use them when the need arises

My wife

My wife is the most important support network I have. I share all my challenges and struggles with her. It can be tough to tell your spouse that you are struggling with fear and anxiety due to the personal recession that you currently face. I see it as a sign of strength. For me, it makes me vulnerable, but because I have invested in our relationship, I can comfortably share what I'm going through with my wife. I'm confident that she will support me. I can confidently say that I always feel much better after speaking with her about my struggles.

If you are married, think about making your spouse one of your support networks. He or she can become a vital asset when you go through personal crises. Depending on the challenges you face, consider how and when to best approach your spouse. If you have had a major relationship issue and you are still healing from it, it may be appropriate to consider whether the timing is good and whether it's appropriate to discuss your struggles. If you don't have a spouse, don't feel like the timing is right or don't wish to discuss your struggles with him or her for whatever reason, then seek support from your other communities.

Spiritual leaders

My wife is my wife, and that is her position in my life. She stands with me during difficult times, but she cannot replace the role of a spiritual leader. Difficulties – especially financial difficulties – can strike the very core of your spiritual being. I have witnessed it myself.

Many years ago, before I got married, I had a relationship issue that began to affect my mind. I was discouraged. I was angry. It began to consume me little by little. I had to do something. I turned to my pastor at the time for help. I set up an appointment and I came out of that meeting refreshed and reinvigorated. We not only talked about my struggles, but we prayed together. This sense of peace came upon me as I left his office. My struggle did not vanish in a flash, but I was able to cope better. I healed faster than I would have on my own.

This is just one example; I have turned to my spiritual leaders on numerous occasions. I have advised, mentored, encouraged, and counselled hundreds of people in the last ten years. Because I know how to give support when someone needs it, I have equally learned how to receive it when I need it myself. Some people are too prideful, ashamed or embarrassed to admit that they need help. Instead, they choose to suffer in silence. Don't be like that. Seek help when you need it, and do it sooner than later. Undoubtedly, there is a place for spiritual support. The spiritual leaders I have had all through my life have supported me through some difficult times. Add yours to your support network and reach out to them when the need arises.

A close friend/family member

A die-hard friend or sibling can be a powerful resource in a time of crisis. I rely on some of my family members and friends for support in times of recession, and there have been times when they stood by my side and held my hands up when I lost all hope of coming out of difficult situations.

About a year ago, I began to doubt and question my purpose in life. For some, this may not be a big deal, but anyone who understands what purpose is knows that doubting your purpose is a big deal. Anyone who does not have a sense of purpose can find it difficult to live and appreciate life. You feel like you are just a wanderer on this earth.

Thanks to a close college friend, I did not get to that point. I called him up and shared with him that I was beginning to doubt my purpose, some choices I had made and God's plan for my life. After sharing my struggles with my friend, he reassured me that my move to a new state was part of God's plan to achieve His ultimate purpose. More importantly, my good friend reminded me that my family, especially my kids, were my purpose. He went on to appreciate how I have raised my kids so far and reassured me that God had great plans for me. Indeed, I was in a crisis, and God used a friend to come to my rescue.

We all need this type of a friend in our lives. If you don't have one, now is the time to find one. It might take time to build and mature, but you have to invest in it. Once you have someone that you share common interests or ideology with in a lot of areas, make time to talk as often as possible. Do things together. Share experiences together. If you are a praying person, pray together. I guarantee you that sooner or later that friendship will grow stronger. You never know when you will need the support.

Professional counsellor

You should add a professional counsellor to the list of your support network. Obviously, it costs money to seek professional help, but it might be worth the price. If you are struggling with addiction, mental illness or any personal trauma, a professional counsellor can help you in your journey to recovery.

A small group

I am a firm believer that many hands can make the load lighter. This couldn't be truer when it comes to finding support during tough times such as a personal financial crisis. My family's church has a small group of people who normally meet once a week. When we gather, we eat, chat, laugh together, and talk about the love of God. The environment creates an opportunity to bond with other people. We encourage and pray for one another.

I regard the individuals in my small group as my second family. Some of my kids went through some health challenges a while ago, during which I found tremendous support from my second family. They not only prayed for us, but they encouraged us and shared some helpful information that helped my family manage the difficult health situations. It would have been hard to navigate some of the struggles had we not received that support. You need this type of support group in your life. If you can't find one, why not start a small group and invite a handful of people?

A group of close friends

I have a group of close friends that I met during my college years. The majority of us attended the same university as well as same campus organizations. We still keep in touch with each other and meet once a month for about an hour to chat. When we meet, we exchange pleasantries, make jokes, laugh. We do life together.

I have benefited tremendously from my college buddies. When my kids were born, I received financial support from them. When I have a question or a challenge that keeps me up at night, my college friends are one of the groups I reach out to. We stay active throughout the month via text messages and social media.

Life is a lot easier to navigate if you have a reliable and strong community that celebrates with you when you excel in life, empathizes with you when you are in pain, lifts you up when you are down, and holds your hand when you are weary and ready to give up.

I hope my personal support networks and their benefits have given you some idea of the types of community that you need to be a part of now. I also hope that you can clearly see why having a community is important. Unfortunately, recessions can bring untold hardships. They are undesirable but inevitable. You can't wish them away, but you can beat them. It all starts by having solid plans in place to control how they impact your life. They will come, but they don't have to derail your life. Building a strong community is a sure way to ensure your survival the next time recession comes.

NOTES

Chapter 1

1. Evie Liu, "What Is A Recession, and How Far Off Is the Next One?," *Barron's*, March 10, 2020, https://www.barrons.com/articles/what-is-a-recession-51583808661.
2. Claire Margerison-Zilko et al., "Health Impacts of the Great Recession: A Critical Review," *National Institutes of Health*, February 3, 2016, https://www.ncbi.nlm.nih.gov/pmc/articles/PMC4880023/.
3. Ibid
4. Ibid
5. Ibid
6. The Wall Street Journal, "Dow Jones Industrial Average," *WSJ Markets*, April 29, 2020, https://www.wsj.com/market-data/quotes/index/US/DJIA.

Chapter 2

1. YouTube, "How to earn money on YouTube," *YouTube Help*, Accessed April 20, 2020, https://support.google.com/youtube/answer/72857?hl=en.
2. Ryan Robinson, "How to Start a Blog in 2020 (and Make Money): Easy Guide to Start Blogging Today," *RYAN ROBINSON*, May 14, 2020, https://www.ryrob.com/how-start-blog/.
3. Barbara Weltman, "SOLE PROPRIETORSHIPS CONTINUE TO INCREASE IN NUMBERS," *BIG IDEAS for Small Business,* May 30, 2019, https://bigideasforsmallbusiness.com/sole-proprietorships-continue-to-increase-in-numbers/.
4. AllBusiness.com, "Advantages and Disadvantages of Sole Proprietorships," *The New York Times*, June 5, 2007,

https://archive.nytimes.com/www.nytimes.com/allbusiness/AB4113314_primary.html?ref=smallbusiness.

5. Nolo, "Sole Proprietorship Basics," Assessed May 29, 2020, https://www.nolo.com/legal-encyclopedia/sole-proprietorship-basics-29694.html.
6. IRS, "Limited Liability Company (LLC)," April 6, 2020, https://www.irs.gov/businesses/small-businesses-self-employed/limited-liability-company-llc.
7. Heather R. Johnson, "What is an LLC (Limited Liability Company)?," *LegalZoom,* May 2019, https://www.legalzoom.com/articles/what-is-a-limited-liability-company-llc.
8. Ibid.
9. Upcounsel, "General Partnership: Everything You Need to Know," Accessed July 7, 2020, https://www.upcounsel.com/general-partnership.
10. Ibid.
11. Will Kenton, "General Partner," *Investopedia*, May 6, 2019, https://www.investopedia.com/terms/g/generalpartner.asp#:~:text=A%20general%20partner%20is%20one,permission%20of%20the%20other%20partners.
12. Nonso E. Okpala, *Financial and Managerial Accounting Key Principles Made Easy* (Cognella, 2016).
13. Legal Information Institute, "Corporations," *Cornell Law School*, Accessed June 14, 2020, https://www.law.cornell.edu/wex/corporations.
14. IRS, "Forming a Corporation," June 12, 2020, https://www.irs.gov/businesses/small-businesses-self-employed/forming-a-corporation.
15. Jim Woodruff, "Advantages and Disadvantages of the Corporate Form of Business," *Chron,* March 4, 2019, https://smallbusiness.chron.com/advantages-disadvantages-corporate-form-business-4389.html.

16. IRS, "S Corporations," April 8, 2020, https://www.irs.gov/businesses/small-businesses-self-employed/s-corporations.

Chapter 4

1. R.L. Adams, "50 Ideas for a Lucrative Side Hustle," *Entrepreneur*, Accessed May 16, 2020, https://www.entrepreneur.com/article/293954.

Chapter 5

1. Michelle F Davis, "JPMorgan Keeps Bonuses Flat for Bankers, Traders," *Bloomberg*, January 27, 2020, https://www.bloomberg.com/news/articles/2020-01-27/jpmorgan-is-said-to-keep-bonuses-flat-for-bankers-traders.
2. Dan Ennis, "Banks cut nearly 78K jobs in 2019, a 4-year high," *Banking Dive*, Jan. 2, 2020, https://www.bankingdive.com/news/banks-job-cuts-2019-4-year-high/569695/.
3. Maurie Backman, "You don't need that: Average American spends almost $18,000 a year on nonessentials," *USA TODAY*, May 7, 2019, https://www.usatoday.com/story/money/2019/05/07/americans-spend-thousands-on-nonessentials/39450207/.
4. Cameron Huddleston, "Survey: 69% of Americans Have Less Than $1,000 in Savings," *Banking Rates*, December 16, 2019, https://www.gobankingrates.com/saving-money/savings-advice/americans-have-less-than-1000-in-savings/.
5. Zack Friedman, "78% Of Workers Live Paycheck To Paycheck," *Forbes*, January 11, 2019, https://www.forbes.com/sites/zackfriedman/2019/01/11/live-paycheck-to-paycheck-government-shutdown/#37ed8beb4f10.

Chapter 6

1. Samiha Khanna, "Debt is causing Americans significant stress and anxiety," *Journal of Accountancy*, December 5, 2017, https://www.journalofaccountancy.com/news/2017/dec/debt-causing-stress-and-anxiety-201717982.html.
2. Joe Resendiz, "Average Credit Card Debt in America: May 2020," *Value Penguin*, July 15, 2019, https://www.valuepenguin.com/average-credit-card-debt.
3. Bob Sullivan, "7 million Americans lost their homes during the recession. Are they ready to buy again?," *BOBSULLIVAN.NET*, April 24, 2015, https://bobsullivan.net/restless/7-million-americans-lost-their-homes-during-the-recession-are-they-ready-to-buy-again/.
4. Environmental and Protection Agency, "Statistics and Facts," Assessed May 24, 2020, https://www.epa.gov/watersense/statistics-and-facts.
5. Joe Roberts, "Utility Bills 101: Tips, Average Costs, Fees, and More," *Move.org*, May 8, 2020, https://www.move.org/utility-bills-101/.
6. Environmental and Protection Agency, "Statistics and Facts," Assessed May 24, 2020, https://www.epa.gov/watersense/statistics-and-facts.
7. Samiha Khanna, "Debt is causing Americans significant stress and anxiety," *Journal of Accountancy*, December 5, 2017, https://www.journalofaccountancy.com/news/2017/dec/debt-causing-stress-and-anxiety-201717982.html.

Chapter 7

1. Ecclesiastes 10:19 English Standard Version
2. Les Christie, "Foreclosures up a record 81% in 2008," *CNN Money*, January 15, 2009,

https://money.cnn.com/2009/01/15/real_estate/millions_in_foreclosure/.
3. US Bureau of Statistics, "Table A-12. Unemployed persons by duration of unemployment," May 11, 2020, https://www.bls.gov/news.release/empsit.t12.htm.
4. Ismat Mangla, "How Much Should You Save Each Month?," *Experian*, May 3, 2019, https://www.experian.com/blogs/ask-experian/how-much-should-you-save-each-month/.
5. Cameron Huddleston, "Survey: 69% of Americans Have Less Than $1,000 in Savings," *Banking Rates*, December 1+6, 2019, https://www.gobankingrates.com/saving-money/savings-advice/americans-have-less-than-1000-in-savings/

Chapter 8

1. Joshua Rosenthal, *Integrative Nutrition: A Whole-Life Approach to Health and Happiness* (New York: Integrative Nutrition, 2019).
2. Markus M. Greffin, "Sitting for long hours reduces blood flow to the brain," *HTQ*, Accessed May 17, 2020, https://healthtopquestions.com/sitting-for-long-hours-reduces-blood-flow-to-the-brain/.
3. ScienceDaily, "Sitting is bad for your brain -- not just your metabolism or heart," April 12, 2018, https://www.sciencedaily.com/releases/2018/04/180412141014.htm.
4. Camille Peri, "10 Things to Hate About Sleep Loss," *WebMD*, February 13, 2014, https://www.webmd.com/sleep-disorders/features/10-results-sleep-loss#1.
5. James McIntosh, "Fifteen benefits of drinking water," *Medical News Today*, July 16, 2018, https://www.medicalnewstoday.com/articles/290814.

6. Ibid.
7. Dminder, "DID YOU KNOW THAT 80% OF AMERICANS ARE VITAMIN D DEFICIENT?," Accessed May 3, 2020, http://dminder.ontometrics.com/about.html.
8. Ansley Hill, "7 Effective Ways to Increase Your Vitamin D Levels," *Healthline*, March 17, 2019, https://www.healthline.com/nutrition/how-to-increase-vitamin-d.
9. Dr. Mercola, "Vitamin D and K2 Work in Tandem to Slow Arterial Calcification," *Mercola.com*, October 19, 2013, https://articles.mercola.com/sites/articles/archive/2013/10/19/vitamin-d-vitamin-k2.aspx.
10. Ansley Hill, "7 Effective Ways to Increase Your Vitamin D Levels," *Healthline*, March 17, 2019, https://www.healthline.com/nutrition/how-to-increase-vitamin-d.
11. Jim Clifton, "The World's Broken Workplace," *Gallup*, June 13, 2017, https://news.gallup.com/opinion/chairman/212045/world-broken-workplace.aspx?g_source=position1&g_medium=related&g_campaign=tiles.
12. Ibid.

Chapter 9

1. Only the Bible.com, "Footprints in the Sand," April 26, 2010, onlythebible.com/Poems/Footprints-in-the-Sand-Poem.html.
2. I heard the story on American Family Radio.

Chapter 10

1. Dan Buettner, *Blue Zones: Lessons for Living Longer From the People Who've Lived the Longest* (Washington DC: National Geographic Society, 2008).
2. Ibid.
3. Proverbs 25:19 King James Version.
4. The Phrase Finder, "The meaning and origin of the expression: No man is an island," Assessed May 19, 2020, https://www.phrases.org.uk/meanings/no-man-is-an-island.html.

ABOUT THE AUTHOR

Nonso Okpala is a certified public accountant, finance controller at one of the leading financial institutions, an integrative nutrition health coach, and a former accounting professor. Nonso has used his expertise as a CPA to help several individuals and small business owners improve their finances. As a health coach, he leverages his blog and social media platforms to create an awareness about holistic and healthy living. Through one-on-one coaching and group presentations, Nonso helps individuals improve their health and discover how to live healthy, be healthy and stay healthy. His other passions include gardening and creating healthy recipes at home. Nonso lives in Delaware, United States with his wife and three beautiful kids, and can be reached online at www.ktvahealth.com.

Connect with Nonso:

* Health Coaching:

Email: **info@ktvahealth.com**
Twitter: **@ktvahealth**
Facebook: **@ktvahealth**
Instagram: **@ktvahealth**

* Author page

Twitter: **@Nonso_Author**
Facebook: **@NonsoAuthor**
Instagram: **@nonso_author**

ACKNOWLEDGMENTS

Writing a book is an arduous task; it is an impossible mission if you do not have the right support. First, I give thanks to God for His wisdom and strength to complete this book.

I would like to express my profound and sincere appreciation to everyone who helped to make this dream a reality. To Dr. Carl Wright, Dr. Thomas Phillips, TJ Sylvis, and Dr. Tobe Momah, thank you for reviewing the manuscript and for recommending this book. It means a lot to me. I greatly appreciate your contributions to my success.

To Blaze Wabo, a brother from another mother, you are truly a special gift to me. Thank you for your continuous support, dating back to our college days. You have stood beside me, even in the nastiest personal recessions that I have experienced. Thank you for your unending support. Your timely feedback and suggestions helped steer this book in the right direction. To Taiwo Stevenson and Kazim Abbot, another good friends who shared feedback on the manuscript, thank you.

To Dr. Janet Guyden, what can I say? I am forever grateful for your candid feedback and suggestions. You helped me to see areas of the manuscript that needed to be strengthened and improved.

Special thanks to my editor, Amanda Lien, for editing and refining the manuscript. To the book cover designer, Sam Art Studio, thank you for being patient, thorough and more importantly, thank you for designing an eye-catching book cover. You rock!

To Men of Purpose, "Bad Brothers", thank you for helping me narrow down and choose the winning book cover. You always push me to accomplish my purpose in life, and to never give up.

I am eternally grateful to my immediate and extended family. You have showered me with love, care, and support. Thank you, Chukwuma "Afunwa" Okpala. You are my backbone.

To Pastor Bryan Smith, I can't thank you enough for not only being my spiritual leader for many years, but also taking me as your own son. I am grateful for your spiritual, moral and material support. Thank you to my former and current church family for your prayers, love, and encouragement. Pastor Mark Lashey and LifeHouse Church, I appreciate your immense support and prayers.

This book would not have seen the light of day without the support from all the mentors and godfathers in my life. Thank you Datin Combs, Dr. Cynthia Warrick, Eric Moses, Harry Malone, Dr. Jan Jasper, Dr. John Nwoha, Dr. Joe Omolayole, Dr. Lawrence Gulley, and many others for believing in me, even when I doubted myself sometimes. Thank you, Michael Holt for pushing me to be the best.

Also, to all my friends and family who are committed to supporting the launch of this book, I am thankful for you sharing the much-needed message in this book to your friends, community, audience, and through your platforms. You are part of the success story; I am grateful for your incredible support.

Finally, my appreciation goes to all my former students, friends, former and current colleagues. As I think about it now, you helped to make me a better person. You are part of my story and success. Without you, my story will be incomplete.

Personal Notes

Personal Notes

Personal Notes

Personal Notes

Personal Notes

Made in the USA
Middletown, DE
05 November 2026

36543429R10088